SHIP TO SHORE

SHIP TO SHORE

FIVE YEARS IN THE 1950S

Hazel Hutchinson

Published by Northsea Publishing

A CIP catalogue record for this book is available from the British Library.

ISBN 978-1-7399814-0-2

Book layout and cover design by Clare Brayshaw

Prepared and printed by:

York Publishing Services Ltd
64 Hallfield Road
Layerthorpe
York YO31 7ZQ

Tel: 01904 431213

Website: www.yps-publishing.co.uk

CONTENTS

PROLOGUE

I have always known about the letters.

When we were children, my brother Michael and I carefully cut out sections of the envelopes and soaked them to remove the foreign stamps, which we then secured with stamp hinges to the appropriate pages of our stamp albums. There were stamps from all around the world: Australia, India, South Africa, South America, North America and the Middle East.

My father was in the Merchant Navy and for five years, from 1953 to 1958, he exchanged letters with my mother. Completely jumbled up by our stamp collecting activities, the letters were stored in a rather battered old suitcase, which moved with my parents whenever they moved to a new house.

After my mother died in 2013, I was clearing her house when I found the suitcase of letters. I began the slow process of putting them into chronological order, first by year, then by month and finally by date. And then I read them.

What emerged was not only a love story but a window into another world.

Memories of the Second World War were fresh in people's minds. Men still had to complete a period of National Service, and many women were members of the women's branches of the Royal Navy, the British Army and the RAF. Post-war food rationing did not end until 1954, while there were still restrictions on buying coal. Most houses had air-raid shelters at the end of their gardens. Many Britons were attracted by the prospect of starting a new life in Australia for a fare of just ten pounds.

Following the Korean War, relationships between the USA and the Soviet Union were extremely tense. Although Stalin died in 1953, the decade saw the formation of the Warsaw Pact and the invasion of Hungary. The Cold War was at its height, with the ideological struggle between capitalism and communism being acted out around the world. When the Suez Crisis erupted in 1956, there were fears that another world war would break out.

It was also the era of Rock and Roll. At the beginning of the decade, the charts were dominated by sentimental ballads, as well as novelty records such as 'How much is that Doggie in the Window'. American records were often re-released by British artists. However, in 1955, 'Rock Around the Clock' by Bill Haley and his Comets became one of the biggest hits in history, after it was used in the film 'The Blackboard Jungle'. Johnny Cash and Elvis Presley had hits with songs including 'Folsom Prison Blues' and 'Heartbreak Hotel'. Lonnie Donegan and other Skiffle bands became very popular in the UK.

The rise of Rock and Roll also influenced fashion. The craze was adopted by Teddy Boys, who were recognised by their drainpipe trousers and bootlace ties. Most men, however, dressed conservatively. Flannel trousers were worn with a shirt and tie, a pullover or sports jacket. Suits were worn for more formal occasions, and trilby hats were the norm when going out. For women, full skirts with tight waists were still popular, but hemlines were gradually getting higher. Stockings were worn with suspender belts and a range of corsetry or 'foundation' garments. More formal occasions demanded hats and gloves, often worn with a 'costume' (a skirt-suit). A fur coat was the ultimate luxury item. Nylon was being used increasingly as a fabric, and the first non-iron shirts were starting to appear.

Ironing was just one of the many household tasks that occupied a nineteen-fifties housewife. Labour-saving devices such as vacuum-cleaners and washing machines were only just being introduced into most homes. Although women had worked outside the home during the Second World War, married women were now encouraged to return to their role as housewives. Cohabiting was rare, being seen as 'living in sin', and most young people would live with their parents until they married. Divorce was difficult, and contraception was only available to married women.

Car ownership was uncommon, and people relied on public transport. Many homes did not have a telephone, so communication with friends and family was often carried out by post, or by simply dropping in to visit. Letter-writing was an essential part of daily life.

Barbara and John's letters began in April 1953, at the start of their whirlwind romance.

John's ports of call around the world

John's ports of call in the United Kingdom, Europe and the Middle East

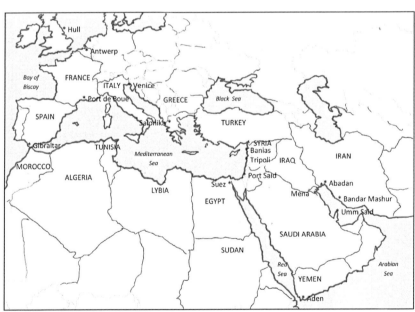

CHAPTER ONE

A WHIRLWIND ROMANCE: MARCH-JULY 1953

'Hold me, thrill me, kiss me' (The Mission, Hull)

Nobody except ourselves can understand how completely and utterly I fell in love with you when we met during that first short break. (John)

Follow the narrow, cobbled street named Posterngate from the Hull Marina to the Minster and you will pass a pub called The Mission. Stepping inside, you will see that it contains a chapel complete with pulpit and stained-glass windows. Founded in 1926 as the Seamen's Mission, this building once provided support and entertainment for seafarers when they were ashore. Barbara's mother, Rhoda, was a volunteer, and Barbara would regularly attend the Friday night dances as a Harbour Light.

A Harbour Light had to make four promises:

(1) never to exchange telephone numbers or addresses with sailors;

(2) never to meet them outside the Mission;

(3) never to accept invitations to ships; and

(4) never to let anyone see her home after mission dances, without permission.

It was here that Barbara met John on Friday 27th March 1953. He was second officer on board MV British Surveyor, an oil tanker owned by the British Tanker Company. His years at sea had given him a dark complexion.

Do you remember darling how I wondered whether you were foreign? You must have thought I was mad when I said "Oh, you're English."

They were both twenty-four. Barbara was five feet two with light brown wavy hair and she was immediately bowled over by this tall handsome stranger:

I am still quite stunned by the way you suddenly came and asked me for a dance, and at the same time completely stole my heart.

John asked permission to take Barbara home in a taxi, to the house in Hessle, just outside Hull, where she lived with her parents and younger brother. Later, he told her what had been going through his mind:

On the way out to Hessle in the taxi I was longing to hold you tight and kiss you, but I thought you would consider me too quick off the mark.

All that weekend I was thinking about you and wondering whether you would turn up at the Mission on the Sunday. I felt sure you would, but I also wondered how I could contact you if you were unable to go. I think that Sunday settled that we should spend the rest of our lives together. I remember looking at you and visualising you in our home as my wife, and the picture entirely pleased me. It was then that I made up my mind to marry you if you would have me as your husband.

They only had a few days to get to know one another before John went back to sea:

It is queer Barbara that, although we have spent so little time together, I felt certain when I returned to the ship that our love would last forever – don't you feel that way too darling? The first night when we danced together, I fell in love with you, but it was the Sunday when I really became hopelessly in love with you and when I realised that you loved me too. Why is it that although we have only known each other a week I find it impossible to get you out of my mind? (Not that I want to!)

'Getting to know you' (Tynemouth to Port Said)

Over the next three months John and Barbara wrote thirty letters to each other, sharing their day to day experiences, their beliefs, their interests, but most of all their conviction that they had found the person that they wanted to spend the rest of their lives with. Their letters are intensely personal, but at the same time they reflect the world they lived in, the popular culture, politics and concerns of these post-war years, and how they affected ordinary people.

John began by telling Barbara about his childhood and his career so far:

In my younger days we had a shop in Beverley selling newspapers and stationery, but business didn't go too well and when I was about ten, we had to give it up and it was then we moved to our present address. Shop-keeping never did interest me but was much more in my brother's line. Nobody in our family had ever been to sea and up to that time I had never liked the water much either (perhaps it was just the washing part of it). Anyhow as I grew older, I began to take an interest in shipping and aircraft, and after a while I combined the two and decided I wanted to enter the Fleet Air Arm. At the age of thirteen I passed a scholarship for the Hull Nautical School and eventually was evacuated to Wakefield, where the school had been moved for the duration of the war. I was there three years, the first two being spent in a billet and the last one in a hostel.

While I was at school my views gradually changed to favour a job that would offer more security in peacetime, and I eventually chose the Merchant Navy. As the time neared for going to sea, my excitement grew, so when I was offered the post of an apprentice in the Bankline, I gladly accepted, knowing that the Bankline went to all parts of the world. Luckily for me we saw little or no action during the war, although at the end of the war we were one of the ships earmarked for the invasion of Malaya.

The only drawback I found with the Bankline, which was managed by Andrew Weir and Co, was the length of the trips. My first trip lasted nineteen months and the subsequent ones were each two years. After I had obtained my Second Mate's ticket, they offered me a position as Second Mate on one of their trips running from South Africa, but once again the trip lasted two years. Thus, after I had obtained my First Mate's ticket, I started looking round for shorter trips.

Eventually I came to the British Tanker Company, where the trips, although not short, are certainly far less than two years. Now I have been in this company's ships for over two years so after I have obtained my Master's ticket, I shall have to decide whether to stay with them or not.

Now you know almost as much about myself as I do, and I don't know what I shall find to talk about when I come home. Anyhow perhaps we can find other uses for our lips; for I long to feel the soft touch of your lips on mine once more. Perhaps I have never told you how nicely you kiss – but you do you know.

Barbara responded by describing how she had always lived in the same street in Hessle, had passed a scholarship to Beverley High School and then worked in a bank:

> But I had only been there eighteen months when the men started coming out of the Services and we younger ones "got the push."

She went on to work as a secretary for a wine and spirit merchant and then for Northern Dairies. Her father was a trolley bus driver, and her nineteen-year old brother Donald was serving three years in the Royal Artillery. Her other brother and sister were both married:

> So that in brief is my history to date. To add just a little more – in March this year I met a very nice young man, tall with blue eyes, who is in the Merchant Navy and I fell madly in love with him, and I am now longing for his return so that I can get to know him better, but I am quite sure I shall always love him, and I hope he feels that way too.

Neither of them commented particularly on their experiences of growing up during the Second World War. Barbara's family used to shelter in the cupboard under the stairs during air-raids, while John's used to huddle under the dining table. Both families preferred not to use their air-raid shelters, despite the intensive bombing of Hull and the surrounding area. John used to wander the fields around Beverley, before he was evacuated, collecting shrapnel and souvenirs. They must have taken these wartime experiences for granted.

As well as sharing their life stories, they shared details of their day-to day activities. Barbara described life in the Administrative Office of the Northern Dairies Group:

> There are approximately thirty people in the office. The Group itself stretches from Teesside, in The North, to Mansfield and Nottingham, in The South, and takes in all the east side of England. There are approximately 2,000 employees, so you will understand why we at Head Office are considered 'rather important'.

> Besides the Directors' Offices, the Accounts section, a typists' room and the general office, there is one very important room which is unofficially referred to as the Fixing Department, and it is here that I work with a very pleasant middle-aged gentleman called Mr Milner. He is in control of all the sales throughout the group, organises such extras as cream, curd, yoghurt, etc.

and is in charge of the Group Welfare Organisation, besides being editor of our very new magazine 'The Northerner'. At the moment, I am working hard to get our third issue out by Easter. It is run off on a Roneo duplicating machine, and so we have quite a lot to do to get it into print. Apart from the usual secretarial work, I also spend quite a lot of time on Sales Statistics, and occasionally some very confidential work for the Chairman of the Group. So, as you can see, I have quite a lot of variation in my work.

Barbara had never travelled abroad, while John had sailed around the world five times. He painted a picture of the places he passed through as the MV British Surveyor sailed from Tynemouth to Port Said:

I always like the journey up a river, but by no stretch of the imagination could the banks of the Tyne be described as picturesque. Along both banks are numerous shipbuilding and repair-works, each yard mothering its dozen or so ships in various stages of completion or repair. In between the various works lies the usual debris of an industrial area – derelict cranes and machinery, coal wharves and loading appliances which have fallen into disuse since the pre-war years, and here and there the skeletal framework of a ship in the breaking-up yards.

He described '*dodging the bad weather in the North Sea*' and '*ploughing through the Bay of Biscay*' before reaching Gibraltar:

Last night we passed, for several hours, great bands of luminescence on the surface of the sea, although at that time there was no moon or stars to be reflected in the water. Tonight, no doubt we shall pass through shoals of dolphins which always seem to congregate in the Straits of Gibraltar.

From Gibraltar the ship made good progress through the smoother Mediterranean:

Thus, we have left behind the highly cultivated coastlands of Tunisia and Eastern Algeria, the dark high misty outline of Pantelleria Island, and the low dark silhouette of Malta.

Eventually they reached Port Said at the entrance to the Suez Canal:

Our berth was just opposite the canal company's offices – a magnificent imposing building surmounted by three domes, each inlaid with varicoloured mosaic work. The harbour was crowded with ships of all nationalities: troopships, every inch of deck space crowded with soldiers; emigrant and passenger ships, practically empty on their way back from Australia; and finally, numbers of tankers like ourselves, each squatting low in the water with its full cargo of oil from the Persian Gulf.

He then describes the overnight passage through the Suez Canal:

To enable us to transit the canal during darkness, a searchlight is mounted on the bow of each ship and a batch of from ten to fifteen ships leave each end of the canal twice daily. We have the honour of being the first ship in a convoy (a position reserved I believe for the slowest ship). The Suez Canal is not so interesting as for instance the Panama Canal, for the eastern bank is an almost continuous stretch of desert broken only by dark masses of boulders. The western side is however irrigated by canals drawing water from the Nile so that there are several patches of greenery. It is along this bank that most of the British troops are stationed and we have passed a number of their camps.

Now we are at last rid of the vendors which swarmed aboard in Port Said. They try to sell you every conceivable thing, trying to convince you of the concessions in price which they are willing to allow you, even adopting the relevant local dialect to try to convince you of their sincerity. Most of them are pure Arab or Egyptian but have adopted English business names, two of the more prominent being George Robey and Hamish McTavish. Most of the goods they sell are rubbishy, but I did buy fresh stocks of writing paper for I can see I shall need them this trip.

'Somewhere Along the way' (Port Said to Mena-al-Ahmadi)

At Port Said, John received his first two letters from Barbara. He had managed to post one to her before leaving Tynemouth and had asked her about her likes and dislikes. Barbara replied:

There are far more things that I like than those I dislike. I quite enjoy life, even though I have not done anything exceptional, but I think it is the small everyday things that contribute most to one's happiness.

Barbara's letters are full of the pleasure she derived from everyday things: cooking for her family, caring for her nieces, buying a new hat, brushing and combing the family collie, or taking a walk in a park.

John's voyage continued through the Red Sea towards Kuwait:

This morning we are sweltering in the centre of the Red Sea, where the temperature is hovering around the 90-degree mark. To add to this, we are at present stopped so we shall be glad when we start moving again and get some breeze. I have just been along to the stern of the ship to see how the shark-fishing is going on but apparently there are none around today. The last time we stopped in the Red Sea the Boatswain caught one some 7 or 8 feet long. We certainly noticed the difference in the weather after passing through the canal, for the Mediterranean was not a lot warmer than England. However, we have a swimming bath rigged up so that the warm weather is quite bearable. It has a disadvantage however in as much as it makes you feel lazy and one can easily spend many hours just sunbathing.

The Suez Canal always makes such a welcome break in the voyage. At last they seem to be getting a few modern appliances for repairing the banks of the canal. On previous trips, it was not uncommon to see hundreds of labourers, each carrying a basket of rubble on his head, proceeding in long snake-like lines from the rubble dumps to the part of the canal being repaired. At various points along the canal you pass Arab villages – mud huts with no roofs, and holes for windows and doors. Around each hut is a small patch of cultivated ground where the owner grows vegetables, and in between the plots wander the village's camels, donkeys and asses.

It is these little things, I think, which make foreign ports so interesting. In fact, I derive a lot of enjoyment out of going ashore in a foreign port and just wandering through the town and surrounding countryside watching people, their ways and the things that happen round about. Very often you learn more in this way than by rushing off on a pre-selected sightseeing tour.

We arrived at Suez just before dusk and without delay our searchlight and boats were lowered into the water and floated away. As night dawned, we steamed slowly south between the great Egyptian plateau on our right and the mountainous Sinai Peninsula on our left. On our way down the Red Sea we pass several isolated islands and reefs, each with its lighthouse, and it makes you think what a lonely life the keepers must have, some of them over a hundred miles from the nearest town.

A few days later, they passed around the extreme eastern point of Arabia:

We passed quite close to the land and were able to see the towers of the various forts which seem to form an integral part of each Arab village. It is here where the roaming Bedouin tribesmen ride, and each village has to be prepared for an attack from them at short notice.

We also passed a number of Arab sailing craft, some packed with passengers and some towing lines to collect sharks. One boat we passed had a shark alongside almost as long as the boat itself.

Before reaching Mena-al-Ahmadi in Kuwait, on April 28th, the ship ran into a sandstorm:

Of course, a sandstorm thirty miles from land isn't half as bad as it would be in the desert, but even so the sand gets everywhere, especially into your eyes. It also makes it impossible to see where we are, but that is when the Radar comes in handy.

There is very little to go on shore for in Mena and, in any case, there is no time. At one time all drinking water had to be brought in there by tanker, but now a massive distillation unit – the largest in the world – distils sea water both for drinking and watering the vegetable gardens. Should you want to keep a flower garden in this part of the world it is necessary to plant all your flowers in pots. Then, on the approach of a swarm of locusts the whole garden is moved indoors, and all the doors and windows closed tightly. While we were loading our cargo this time, quite a number of locusts, like great flying grasshoppers, were flying around, along with multi-coloured dragonflies.

'Faith can move Mountains' (Mena-al-Ahmadi)

Waiting at Mena were two more letters from Barbara. She described how she had just finished '*a most fascinating book*' called Light over Fatima'

It is based on the unusual incidents in Fatima (Portugal) in 1917, when three children had several visits by the Virgin Mary, who foretold that there would be a great turn against the church especially in Russia, which has been proved by the birth and rapid growth of Communism. I do not know whether you have read anything on this subject, but to me, although some of the things seem a little too imaginative, I am convinced that there is a certain amount of truth in the story. Lately I have done quite a lot of reading on similar lines, about comparatively modern saints, and I must admit, apart from any question of belief or faith, they certainly give one quite a lot to think about, and I find they are equally as good and interesting as the average fiction books. Some time I should like to read a good book on Comparative

Religions, for I think one can very easily say that they believe their way is best without knowing much about the others. I try to be quite open-minded on the subject, whilst sticking firmly to the Church of England.

Tonight, of course, I shall be going to the Mission. It seems hard to believe that a fortnight ago at this time I did not know you existed darling, and yet I now I feel as though I have known you a very long time (except when I write about such things as religion when I do not know your views and I may be 'rushing in where angels fear to tread').

Barbara need not have worried. John was more than willing to share his beliefs:

Religion is a subject which is taboo at sea. However, it is such an important subject that it should be talked about freely. Before I came to sea I was quite a staunch C of E churchgoer, but of course at sea Sunday is just like any other day unless we listen to the church service on the radio. So far, I have sailed in ships having Chinese, Malayan and Indian crews so I have come up against several different religions. Many of these natives were just as sincere and more devoted in their religion than most Europeans are to the Christian religion. This made me interested in the comparative study of the various religions and I was surprised at the amount they had in common. Much as certain points in their religions appealed to me, none of them seemed to fit fully into the world around, and all of them were cloaked in mysticisms which I found impossible to believe. Turning back to the Christian religion, the diversities of opinion between the various factions in the Church first struck me. Surely, I thought, there can be only one true religion and one true theology. For a while I studied the Catholic viewpoint but to me symbolism takes on too strong a form and although their services are picturesque and full of meaning, I preferred a service I could take a full part in, with few or no abstract ceremonies. Thus, although I am a member of the Church of England, my beliefs tend towards those of the Congregationalists. Even so, I try to maintain an open viewpoint, for I realise how much our views are coloured by our upbringing and our environment.

Barbara and John both came from religious families. Barbara mentioned that she was a Sunday School teacher and John replied that Sunday School teaching had a romantic connection in his family, as his mother and father had met through being teachers at the same church. John went on to enlarge on his religious beliefs:

Many people nowadays say they can get on without religion but to me it appears to be essential in order to lead a full life. In fact, I could say it is more important to believe in a god than which god you have faith in. The majority of religions seem to have a similar moral code and it would seem to me that religions growing up in such widely separated places, and at a time when communication between different parts of the world was bound to be on a small scale, would develop along different lines.

I have noticed too how much the Christian faith has been interpreted in different forms by people of different races and temperaments. Each religion has its different rites and ceremonies, the majority of which to me are purely symbolic. Thus, to me Heaven and Hell also appear symbolic and do, I believe, represent a person's state of happiness on this earth. Happiness seems to me to be a thing which depends almost wholly on a person's state of mind. Given faith and a lively interest, even a person living in miserable circumstances can be happy. Perhaps I should hold a different view had I lived in dire circumstances or poor health, for no doubt my views are coloured by my surroundings. As for the life hereafter, it has always appeared difficult to me to visualise life in the world to come and how our spirits and bodies would separate or come together. Eventually I came to the conclusion that your spirit is being passed on every day of your life. Every action you take and everything you do has an influence on the people round about you either good or bad. Therefore, I consider that when a person dies his spirit has already been passed on to the people he has been in contact with during his life.

No doubt by the time you have read this you are brimming over with objections, and I too have found many objections which the above does not seem to supply a satisfactory answer to. Perhaps in the future I may change my views, for I try to be open-minded and have a tolerant if not sympathetic view towards other ideas. Maybe by now you think I am a religious outcast or a crank, but I have tried to show you how I differ from the orthodox view. I do believe in the power of prayer and I go to church because I want to, not because I think I ought to. Anyhow that is enough theorising for the present and now to get on to more mundane subjects.

'Till I waltz again with you' (The Persian Gulf)

Day-to-day life on board ship certainly included some mundane domestic tasks, as well as the more technical ones:

I must be up bright and early (before breakfast anyhow) for it is dhobi-day and I have a great pile of washing to wade through as well as the subsequent ironing. The company put several washing machines on board, so I can usually sandwich the washing in between checking the ship's position at 9.30 am and going on watch at midday.

John's domestic talents did not extend to cooking:

Quite a lot of seamen can cook too, to a limited extent, but it is one thing that I leave severely alone.

He was however adept at multitasking:

I am one of those people who, perhaps fortunately, can either write or read a book while at the same time listening to the radio.

He described how he would listen to Listeners' Choice (both light and classical versions), Henry Cotton's Band Show, Ray's-a-laugh, and the science reviews:

In this part of the world some of the stations broadcast sponsored music and, although I like it for a change, I soon get tired of the constant repetition of the current song hits.

What song hits would he have been listening to in April-May 1953? One of the most popular songs was 'How Much is that Doggie in the Window?'. The recording by Lita Roza reached No 1 on the UK singles chart and was the first number one UK hit by a British woman. I remember my mother still singing this song, when I was growing up in the 1960s. John may have also listened to 'Till I Waltz Again with You', which was number one in the USA and even sung by Elvis Presley for his high-school talent show in April 1953. It was recorded in the UK by Alma Cogan and Joan Regan. Surely the lyrics of this song would have evoked for John the memory of dancing with Barbara the night they met at the Mission, and the promise of being reunited.

For the moment, Joan and Barbara just had their letters and photographs. They exchanged photographs, although both had doubts about how they would be received.

As promised, I will have a photograph taken specially for you John, although I am not a very photogenic person, and most of my photographs make me look extremely sad or 'all teeth'!

John replied by saying that most of the photos taken of him from the front don't look too bad, *'but if you see one taken from the side you would probably disown me.'*

Their words however continued to fan the flame of their romance:

My dream girl has blue eyes, bewitching lips, an enchanting smile and a sense of humour combined with a capacity for being serious at the right times. For her other characteristics you could look in a mirror or try some self-analysis. I hope it won't be long before I see my dream girl again but until then I must be content with her letters – and my dreams.

John left the hot, dry port of Mena, and the British Surveyor steamed through the damp, oppressive heat of the Persian Gulf, passing close to the Sheikh of Kuwait's luxury yacht. Looking back on this time later, John wrote:

The letters I received from you at Mena-al-Ahmadi made me realise that your views were very similar to mine on most important matters. It was then that I really began thinking of getting married and starting a family as soon as possible for I knew that the more days I had with you the happier I should be.

'I Believe' (Crossing the Red Sea to Suez)

Rounding the southern coast of Arabia, John commented on how the monsoon wind *'beside retarding our progress is keeping us nice and cool'*.

They continued through the Red Sea towards Suez, where John eagerly awaited more letters from Barbara. In the meantime, he re-read the ones he had already received, and answered some of her questions in more detail. Barbara had told him that she was a member of the Young Liberals. She wrote:

At one time I was extremely keen on Liberalism and was on several committees, but I am afraid that during the last year my enthusiasm for it has waned. Although I do think the Liberals have the best ideals, I do not think they have sufficient strong people to put these into a really good policy and then push it. I believe that most people are Liberal at heart but are not willing to vote for the Liberal Party because it is not big enough. I suppose it is just a vicious circle really because the Parliamentary Liberal Party will never grow unless people vote for Liberal candidates. I am not anti-Tory or anti-Socialist – I think both have their good points. What are your political views, John? Do you feel strongly about any party?

John's father also regularly attended committee meetings at his local Liberal club, but John was more pragmatic in his political allegiances:

It largely depends on the programme the individual parties put forward at the elections to determine who I vote for now. Despite the small number of successful Liberal candidates at the election, I think they have an influence out of all proportion to their numbers. Unless one of the other parties incorporate Liberal ideas into their programme, I shall no doubt go on supporting the Liberal party, but if, as in many elections, the Liberal candidate has no hope of succeeding may well support either the Socialist or the Conservatives, depending on whose policy I disagree with least.

He then continued to explore his '*views and theories which are not necessarily correct*':

To begin with, I will describe the system of government which I consider would be the most efficient. It would not necessarily be the best and I do not imply by this that I am dissatisfied with the present system in England. As a basis for the Government, I consider that the present party system should remain, but only as policy-making bodies. Each year each party would put forward to the public their programme of legislation for the coming year, in broad principle. This programme would be printed, circulated and advertised by the parties concerned, and each year the relative merits of each would be considered by the general public and voted upon. Whichever programme received the most votes would be the one which would form a basis for laws in the coming year. Should parliament fail to carry it out, the Royal Prerogative would be exercised, and a new parliament would have to be elected. The members of parliament on the other hand would not be elected on a party system but from a personal angle according to their ability. I think one of the great disadvantages of modern politics is that it neglects the personal angle and people vote for the party not the candidate. This is a fault which proportional representation would only intensify. Elections for Parliament could still be held at intervals of four years.

I wonder whether by this time you are up in arms against my theories but in case you are not you may be interested in more of my views. When I say that I consider equal pay for everybody to be a worthwhile ideal, you will probably label me as a Communist, but far from it. Should everybody get equal pay, people would tend to enter the cleaner industries and industries with shorter working hours, with the result that people in other industries would have to work longer and longer hours, thus there would be no tendency to equilibrium. The only answer to this would be Governmental direction of labour, which I consider is a greater evil than unequal wages.

Barbara responded:

Your ideas on government really interest me but I can think of one or two reasons why they would not work, or at any rate more efficiently than the present system. My main objection is that if the political parties were putting forward their programmes every year, which would mean a possible change of programme every year, one might find the situation where, for instance, an industry was nationalised one year, denationalised the next, and nationalised the next. I admit that I am possibly exaggerating, but that type of situation could arise.

I agree with you that one would possibly get a better parliament if MPs were chosen for their personal ability, but of course the present electoral system discourages that. I rather deplore the lack of interest in political affairs by the average person and the low percentage of votes at the poll, but apart from making it compulsory to vote at a general election – as in Australia – I do not quite see what can be done.

I am not so sure about equal pay. Although it sounds a good idea, equal pay for all, I do not think it is so good in practice; and although I agree that there is certainly a need for improvement in the wages of workers, I think in some cases they have gone to the extreme. I think the situation is becoming increasingly common where an unskilled or partly skilled labourer is earning a wage higher than the person who has spent two years extra at school and then several years of study afterwards. For example, a road labourer with no real qualifications can earn about £8 a week, or more with overtime, whereas an accountant, not fully qualified but having studied five or six years and passed several exams, is only getting £6 to £7 a week. On a more personal note, an 18-19-year-old girl in our ice cream factory in the height of the season earns far more than I do, and yet I am a senior secretary on the Group's administration staff and am considered to be getting a good salary. Although I agree that manual work is essential, something seems very wrong somewhere.

Regarding equal pay for women, although I can see the justice of it, I fear that if women have equality with men, and obviously if they want it one way they will have it another, then women will lose out ultimately because they will lose their femininity. I think I would rather be treated with courtesy by the male sex than be just an equal!

Unusually, John was unwilling to comment:

Equal pay for women is an argument I refuse to be drawn into on either side.

He was however encouraged by what he read of Barbara's beliefs and opinions:

When I first fell in love with you darling, I knew so little about you and yet the more I get to know you the greater is my love for you. I was not to know then that we should have so many interests in common, but it is a fact that we do seem to think along the same lines in so many things.

Religion and politics were not the only subjects on which they sought each other's views. John wrote:

By the way, do you feel strongly about alcohol? My attitude towards it is similar to my attitude towards smoking. Where it helps to create an easier and friendlier atmosphere it has its uses, but where it becomes a habit or even a necessity then it should be strongly avoided. On board the ship or in foreign ports I sometimes have the odd beer, and when the captain calls me up to his room for a drink it certainly isn't possible to refuse. When home however it is only on special occasions or when we have visitors that we take the bottle out. You certainly need have no fear of me getting drunk sometime, for we have enough trouble on board the ship keeping an eye on the sailors when they return drunk.

Barbara's views on alcohol were similar, but hinted at guilty pleasures:

My views on alcohol are very much the same as yours. I will have an occasional drink at a party or similar to be sociable, but I would certainly never go out of my way to have one. When I do drink, however, my tastes are rather expensive. I never have drunk beer, the smell of it puts me off. My favourite drink is sherry. I don't like spirits – except rum sauce in puddings – but I must admit I rather like champagne, and some of the liqueurs. However, there is one thing that I am rather partial to, and that is at a big dinner to have the various wines with each course. I did say that I had expensive tastes!

John was slightly worried by this:

I can see that being the secretary of a wine and spirit merchant has given you expensive tastes in wine. I too like champagne, and also its poor relation, cider. Wines with a meal certainly help to make it, but they also help to make the bill and have to be kept for really special occasions.

On the subject of reading, John expressed a preference for non-fiction *'for stranger things happen in life than are ever conjured up in an author's mind'*. He admitted that he could get completely absorbed in a book and would read deep into the night if it interested him:

Yesterday I just finished a book describing how the various parts of a motor car and its engine worked. Perhaps I have an insatiable curiosity for I can pick up a book on almost any technical subject and become absorbed in it in a very short space of time. It is sometimes said that sailors know a little about everything but not a lot about anything, and there may be some truth in this. You certainly have to be self-contained at sea, being doctor one day and perhaps plumber the next.

John was always trying to expand his knowledge, but some subjects were less absorbing than others:

During my spare time I have been trying to polish up some mathematics, but I find it such a lifeless subject that it is hard to concentrate upon. In this climate however it takes quite an effort to get anything done, so a large proportion of my time off-duty has been spent merely being lazy.

In the heat of the Red Sea, the main leisure activity was swimming in the makeshift pool they had rigged up, but John described how on one ship they marked out a pitch on the deck and played cricket with a homemade bat, a rope and canvas balls. They also had darts tournaments:

Double One seems to be my bugbear and I had nearly fifty tries at it during one game.

'All the Time and Everywhere' (Suez to Venice)

Eventually they reached Suez Bay and dropped anchor while they awaited the night convoy:

The Bay is full of ships, mostly tankers, all flying flags to indicate that they require a pilot and also to indicate whether or not they are carrying dangerous cargoes. We have on board a cargo of crude oil which will no doubt be refined at Venice.

Here in Suez, in the sea around the ship are thousands of jellyfish, which the exceptional clearness of the sea enables us to see. They are a vivid violet and look very beautiful but no doubt they have a powerful sting.

They had a quiet passage through the canal, but John wondered whether it would be the same next time, *'for it looks as if there will be more trouble with the Egyptians sooner or later'*. It would be three years before the Suez Crisis of 1956, but relations between Britain and Egypt had been at a low ebb since the Egyptian government ended the Anglo-Egyptian Treaty in 1951. Britain had refused to withdraw its forces from Suez and there had been anti-Western riots in Cairo.

This was not the only time that national and international events made their presence felt in John and Barbara's letters. When Barbara told John that her younger brother, Donald was travelling to Korea with the Royal Artillery, John replied:

it is a good job things are quieter now in Korea. Let us hope they stay that way. Perhaps the Russians and Chinese are genuinely wanting peace, but I am afraid I am still suspicious of their intentions.

There were two letters from Barbara waiting for John in Suez. In one she said how envious she was of John's travels:

I wish I had the opportunity to travel and see so many different countries, like you do. It must be fun too, to meet the different inhabitants of the various countries. Do you find any difficulty in understanding the foreigners whom you meet, or have you already learnt a little of the various languages?

John replied:

I am afraid languages are not one of my bright subjects, but we find people speaking English in almost any part of the world we go. Of course, we usually pick up a bit of the local language, but it is amazing how much you can explain merely by signs.

Although Barbara may have envied John his travels, she had her own adventures:

On Saturday morning, I arranged to meet one of our Sales Representatives outside Hull Dairies, so that I could collect some fresh cream, which he was getting for me at wholesale price. At the arranged time I arrived at the Dairy but there was no sign of Mr Bolder, although a black Ford car was outside. Presuming Mr Bolder was in the Dairy talking, I sat in the driving seat of the car and gave a few loud hoots on the horn. In a minute or two out came Mr Bolder and I jumped out of the car and went to meet him. I said, "I thought I would sit in the car while I was waiting."

On Monday morning, Mr Milner said to me that he thought I always said I could not drive, so I said that I can't, at least not properly. He refused to believe me and asked, if I could not drive, how did I manage to drive a car on my own to the Dairy on Saturday? He said I could not deny that as George had seen me in a black Ford. Very surprised, I said that of course he had seen me sitting in it, but that was all, and in any case, it was Mr Bolder's car I was sitting in. Mr Bolder then assured us that he had driven his car into the Dairy yard when he arrived, so obviously I had been sitting in a complete stranger's car and hooting his horn. Naturally Mr Milner and Mr Bolder thought it highly amusing and speculated as to what would have happened if the car owner's wife had gone by and seen me sitting in the car – I most certainly will check the car number in future!

After the coasts of Egypt, the next land that John saw was Crete. They navigated by the vague shapes of the mountain peaks of Greece and the off-lying islands, and into the Adriatic Sea. On arrival at Venice, they swam in the sea until the Third Mate mentioned having seen a hammerhead shark last time he was here. After that John noticed a marked reluctance to enter the water around the ship. Instead, they lowered a motorboat and anchored near the beach, swimming in the warm water and watching the crowds sunbathing.

He asked Barbara how she was coming on with her swimming. She had expressed a determination to learn to swim this year, but felt it was too cold to start yet. (She finally managed to swim a width of the pool, in doggy-paddle, in about 1968).

From where they were anchored, John could clearly see the towers, campaniles and domes of Venice. It was unusual for them to spend such a long time in a foreign port, but after a few days they received orders that they were to load in Venice and then sail to Colombo in Ceylon, now Sri Lanka.

'Outside of Heaven' (Venice)

In Venice, there was a letter waiting from Barbara. In it she said how she envied her mother a recent sightseeing and shopping trip to London. She wished she could visit London more often; instead she had to make do with dressing up in her spring clothes and shopping in Hull:

> *I put on my new blue costume and was in search of a hat. I eventually bought one in white straw, with two white roses at the back. I was really quite pleased with it. Tell me, darling, do you prefer your girlfriends with or without hats?*

Never one to dodge a difficult question, John replied diplomatically:

> *Your new hat sounds to be quite a picture but with or without a hat you look nice to me. You ask me whether I like my girlfriends to wear hats, but surely that should be in the singular, for since I met you I have but one girlfriend. To my view, hats are suitable for many occasions and the wearing of a hat should be governed by the occasion – and the weather. In fact, I find I have to wear a hat in windy weather to keep my hair out of my eyes.*

Barbara had been busy editing the Northern Dairies in-house magazine:

> *I have just been working on one article which should be quite amusing when finished but it needs cutting down from 250 words to 150, so I am busy with the blue pencil, crossing out the padding. It is a salutation from the Doncaster office girls to the moustache grown by one of the dairy foremen. According to this article, it has grown quite a lot of admiration from the girls and envy from the men.*

She complained that much of the copy they received was no use at all, '*especially some of the poetry which does not even rhyme.*'

Barbara asked John if he could help her:

> *I have to make up a crossword for the autumn issue, so if that is in your line John I shall be extremely grateful if you can do one for me. I have had one or two attempts but, so far, I can only do about half of one and then I get stuck. We really want one with two or three alternatives, similar to those in the 'People'. So, if you can help darling…*

John was happy to oblige:

> *Since I received your letter I have been trying my hand at crosswords although I have rarely tried solving them before, never mind composing them. After a*

struggle I actually managed to complete one, but I haven't attempted making out clues for it. A thesaurus would no doubt be very useful in determining clues. I have one at home but no doubt you could get one from the library.

Barbara was a member of the Wrens (Women's Royal Naval Service). They were due to have a big inspection by the Admiral Commanding Reserves:

Last Monday we had two hours drilling on the parade ground, with an inspection by our own officers thrown in. Several of us, including myself, were told we had to do something about our hair by next Monday, as it had to be off our collars. I think I shall put mine in a roll, but it makes me look very severe. This year, the Admiral wants everyone to go by in a single column, three yards between each person, and everyone has to salute him. We certainly needed plenty of practice – I have never seen so many peculiar salutes in all my life.

She goes on to reveal that she understands a little of what is involved in John's task of correcting charts:

When the Wrens were taken for our first instructional cruise (to Bridlington) on the minesweeper, the Captain explained to us about the charts and that they were altered quite frequently. We were also given a very brief outline on how to navigate and plot a course.

John responded:

By the time I have written this letter, the Admiral's inspection will have been over, and I hope you brought up your hand at the right angle as you passed him. No doubt drilling is a necessity in the Wrens, but I'm sure the cruises on the minesweepers are much more enjoyable.

He was making the most of his remaining time in port by going ashore and taking the bus into Venice, so that he could paint a picture for Barbara of a place she could only dream of visiting:

The bus took us to the outskirts of Venice, for there are no roads in Venice, the streets being mere alleyways. This means there is no motor traffic, but you still have to watch your step, for streets are liable to end without warning at the brink of a canal.

From the outskirts of Venice, we took the ferry-boat down the Grand Canal to St Mark's Square. Each side of the canal is lined with what used to be the

Palaces of the Nobles of Venice. Now many of them have been converted into hotels, museums, etc, and the faded and peeling facades still hide a grandiose interior.

After a very interesting journey we arrived at St Mark's Square and indeed it was a most impressive place. Due to the absence of roads, it looks more like a courtyard than a square and it is surrounded by magnificent buildings. Its crowning glory is St Mark's Cathedral, but just to the right of that is the Doge's Palace and offset to one side is the 325-foot-high bell tower or Campanile. There was a lift to the top of this tower but as we were still feeling fresh we decided to climb up the stairs, so we could see the view from various heights. When we reached the top, we decided it had been well worth the trouble for the whole of Venice and the surrounding district was laid out before us.

After this we decided to explore other parts of the town and in next to no time we were lost among the maze of alleyways and canals. Still wherever we went we found spectacular architecture and sculpturing and always something to captivate your interest. Eventually we discovered where we were and went on to find the Post Office and do our shopping.

By this time, we were feeling a bit thirsty, so we went into a café and ordered a Coca-Cola. Along came the drink and along too came rolls and a most repulsive-looking piece of cheese. We weren't hungry, so we left the cheese, but when the bill came along, we had been charged for the cheese and all. We couldn't convince the waiter that we didn't want cheese. At first, he thought we hadn't had enough and brought more, then he paraded along with specimens of different types of veined cheese, and finally he was going to wrap us up some particularly strong-smelling cheese to carry round with us for the rest of the afternoon. It was only when I point-blank refused to give him any more money that the cheese disappeared away under the counter.

The ship remained in port a couple more days while loading was finished, and engine repairs carried out. John went ashore again:

A number of small orchestras were playing in St Mark's Square, so we sat down with a cup of coffee and listened to the music. Later the apprentice and I wandered along the banks of the Grand Canal and watched the fairy-tale like gondolas slip by, each lit by coloured lanterns. Now and then a cluster of gondolas would pass, gathered round another on which a musician with a banjo would be singing various airs. It all looked and sounded fascinating and romantic. If only you could have been here, we could have enjoyed it to the full…

'Tell me a Story' (Venice to Port Said)

From the ship's point of view, the stay in Venice had been dogged by mishaps: engine trouble, a fire in the boiler room, a leak in the shell plating, and finally a grounding on mud banks as they attempted to leave the port. As they sailed again for Port Said, John was busy correcting charts and tackling a mountainous pile of washing, as all his gear had got oily and dirty whilst loading and discharging in port. He was thinking again about Barbara and when he might see her again:

> *it was just two months ago today when we last saw each other Barbara, but it seems much longer. Now I know much more about what you do and think than I did then, but it only helps to reinforce my love for you. I have never looked forward so much to my next leave as I am doing now, and I wish I had a better idea of when it is likely to be. It is all very enchanting not knowing where you will be a few weeks hence, but it also means you can't plan far ahead.*

In Port Said, there was a letter from Barbara in which she described her first caravan holiday, with her mother, sister-in-law and niece, at Bridlington on the Yorkshire coast. She was travelling into Hull each day on the train to go to work. John pointed out that she would have seen his home in the last row of houses on the right-hand side as the train left Beverley for Hull. Barbara had neither visited his home nor met his parents at this stage.

Barbara described in detail how the caravan was cleverly designed to convert the living room to a dining room, the sideboard to a kitchen, and the settee to a bed. Despite a couple of cold rainy days, they had managed to spend time on the beach and Barbara had enjoyed long walks along the seafront.

John replied that he too loved long walks and would look forward to spending the long summer evenings walking with Barbara. In response to his comment that he would *'really prefer spending my holidays in a caravan rather than at a hotel,'* she said:

> *Having a rather expensive streak in my makeup, I must admit to getting quite a lot of pleasure from an occasional visit and stay at a big hotel, with lots of service and having no worries – except about paying the bill!*

But she added:

> To me it is far more important that I like the people with whom I am sharing the holiday. I am quite easy to please – or so I think!

John described the continuous flow of tradespeople that came to his cabin when they reached Port Said:

> First, a barber comes along brandishing all the tools of the trade and informs you of the urgent necessity of getting your hair cut. On informing him that you don't require it cutting, he fishes various watches out of his pocket and tries to sell you one of those. This not being successful, other oddments are produced out of his voluminous robes and soon a whole shop is spread out in front of you.
>
> The next man to see you is the 'gilly-gilly' man or conjuror. He comes in and proceeds to produce chickens and what-not out of your shirt and pockets. After a small but convincing display, he produces a magic note and after a few magic words he says that he has found its way into your wallet. On questioning him where the wallet is, he makes a guess, which in my case proved wrong. That ended the display for me, although several times he came back for his magic note, which he said was still in my wallet. Of course, the note never went near my wallet and I for one wasn't trusting such a nimble-fingered Egyptian anywhere near my wallet. Afterwards it transpired that various things had disappeared from other cabins after the gilly-gilly man had been.
>
> These two were just the forefront of the mob that besieged my cabin while I was trying to get an hour or two's shut-eye, and finally I had to give up the idea altogether.

'In a Golden Coach' (Port Said to Ceylon)

They moored opposite a Royal Navy Depot ship which was busy with its preparations for the coronation of Queen Elizabeth:

> On the front of the bridge they have a big card painted 'EIIR' while on top of the bridge they have constructed an enormous crown out of wire, coloured lights and bunting.

June 2nd was Coronation Day. On the following day, Barbara wrote:

Being at the office today seems an anti-climax after the excitement of yesterday. I think it was a day I shall always remember. It started quite early by all our family going to Holy Communion at our church. After breakfast, about 9.50 am, we went round to our friend's house, where we stayed most of the day watching the TV. The Queen looked really lovely and so very young to have such a large responsibility, not that I doubt that she will more than fulfil her duty. It seemed so very symbolic that when the heavy crown of St Edward was placed on her head it seemed to weigh her down, as she sometimes probably feels weighed down with her cares and responsibilities, and yet her quiet dignity and obvious trust in God will always help her. It was a terrible day so far as weather was concerned, raining most of the time and very strong winds, but I am sure no Sovereign could have had a more triumphant ride back to the palace than our Queen had. Despite the weather, everywhere was packed with people, some of whom had camped out since Sunday, and everyone was so happy. No – I am quite sure I shall never forget the Coronation of Queen Elizabeth the Second.

After we returned home in the evening, we listened to a broadcast covering the celebrations throughout the world, before going to bed. I must admit I was rather ready to go, for although the day had been a quiet one physically, mentally it had been very exhausting. Also, I had been dancing until 1.0 am that morning. Monday night we had a special Coronation dance at the Mission from 8.0 pm until 1.0 am, which was quite fun, although I kept wishing you were there with me.

Meanwhile, near Suez, John was listening on the radio:

It was Coronation day when we left Suez, so we spent most of our leisure hours during the day with our ears glued to the radio loudspeakers. We were most fortunate in being near Suez for we were able to hear the BBC relayed through the "Canal Forces Radio Station." The Red Sea is notorious for its bad radio reception and had we been a day further down the Red Sea, I doubt whether we should have picked up most of the ceremonies. As it was I was even able to listen to the radio at times during my afternoon watch for the Chart Room is next to the Radio Cabin and while "Sparks" was "off watch" I was able to have the ship's main receiver tuned in to the BBC. Well from what we heard everything seemed to go smoothly despite the rain so now we are speculating as to whether any of the Coronation films will have reached Colombo by the time we get there.

He continued his account on the 17th June:

I am afraid I haven't much news to tell you about Colombo for we only stayed one and a half days there and it was not until the last night that I was able to go ashore. The film of the Coronation was being shown at one of the local cinemas and a little to my surprise we were able to book a seat. I was well rewarded though, by the magnificent and moving film that followed. It certainly must have been a great strain on the Queen, but she struck me as having an air of quiet confidence in her ability, with the help of God, to fulfil her duties to the full.

Before arriving in Colombo, they had crossed the Red Sea again:

Today the sea is like a sheet of glass, and almost as clear. From the bridge it appears to be a very deep azure blue and it is only when we see the odd fish down in the depths that we realise just how transparent the sea is.

Conditions soon changed, however, once they felt the effects of the south-west monsoon:

As soon as we reached the Arabian Sea, the weather worsened and for the last week we have had nothing but warm, wet and windy weather. Luckily for us the wind has been astern, so it has not held us back very much, but the decks have been continually awash. When the bad weather first set in we managed to catch one or two flying fish which had either been washed or flown on to our decks, but since it worsened we have kept to the upper decks and bridge wherever possible.

There were letters from Barbara waiting at Colombo. She described a church service that she had attended in a local park:

It was a lovely day, warm yet not hot, and the singing of the birds outside blended in with the voices of the congregation and the band. I was struck by the thought that on such a day, outside with nature, we seemed very close to God, despite the crying of some little child in the crowd. I expect you know the feeling. I have often had it when I have been alone in a church, kneeling down, and felt quite sure that I was not alone and that He was there. It is a wonderful feeling and seems to put an extra zest into life.

She had also been selling flags in aid of the Seamen's Mission:

I quite enjoy selling flags – it is fun to watch people trying to avoid me – although I must admit I am usually quite successful. I guess I must have a good approach! Unless people just take pity on me!

Always busy, Barbara had just made herself a new dress, 'green with tiny brown spots, with white trimmings. Her letter included a 'selfie' of herself taken through a mirror.

John commented:

I certainly have never tried photographing myself through a looking glass, but your effort didn't turn out too bad.

After watching the film of the Coronation in Colombo, John walked back to the ship through the native bazaar:

Here all was noise and bustle, each café blaring forth native music through loudspeakers, staunch in the faith that the noisiest café would attract the most customers. Travelling dancing girls with tambourines helped to swell the noise as they travelled down the street giving a performance in front of each shop. Gradually however as I neared the ship the noise subsided, for here in Ceylon few shops stay open after dark, and soon only the rattling of the trams remained to disturb the Asian night.

'Downhearted' (Ceylon to Kuwait)

From Colombo the British Surveyor was heading for Umm Said in Qatar, encountering more bad weather in the Arabian Sea:

For the past four days we have been subjected to winds of gale force and tropical downpours. It is hard to believe that only a few hundred miles on either side of us lie arid deserts parched through lack of rain.

All the leaks and defects seem to show up in bad weather, and this time was no exception. First the Radar went wrong, then the Gyro, and then the deckhead above my bunk started leaking. The faults in the first two were soon remedied, but the leaks turned out to be rather a difficult problem. In the end I had to fit a container below the leaks with a tube leading from it clear of my bunk. Tonight, I hope once more to be able to sleep in my bunk after having spent the last two on the settee.

Navigation has been quite a problem for in cloudy weather we have to rely on the sun, almost exclusively, to give us the ship's position. For the past week the sun has only shown through fitfully once or twice a day and for the last three days we haven't seen it at all. We were due to sight land tonight, so it was with a sense of relief that we saw the sun peeping through this morning. When we calculated our position, we were less than half a dozen miles from where we thought we were, which wasn't bad after a run of over seven hundred miles without checks.

At Umm Said, the pilot brought mail out to the ship, including a long envelope containing photographs and letter from Barbara. Of the photographs, Barbara said:

When I saw the result, and when the family had made their comments, I decided neither was worth having enlarged, so I am sending you both. I hope you are able to recognise them as being me. The dress is the one I made myself a week or so ago.

John replied:

Of the two photos you sent me I think I like the smaller one best, for I like to see you smiling, and besides I think the half-front view usually gives a better picture. The dress you made seems to be a very good fit, although of course I can't see much of it. They are lovely photos but what photos wouldn't be lovely with you as the subject dearest? Perhaps they don't do you credit, but perhaps soon we shall see each other in the flesh again. Only then can I realise to the full what a lucky boy I am to have such an attractive and intelligent girlfriend.

Now that the British Surveyor had been given the destination of 'Land's End for Orders' after Umm Said, there was a one in four chance that they would sail to the UK rather than Hamburg. They might soon be reunited. Barbara wrote:

When I fell in love with you dearest there was no 'half-measure'. I should have thought it impossible to love someone and long for them as much as I do, after such a short time together. I only hope you will not be disappointed in me, darling, when you know me better.

John replied:

I am sure I shan't be disappointed when I get to know you better although I feel I know you very well already. I can hardly believe we had so short a time together, for you left such an impression on me and mean so much to me darling. On the other hand, when you get to know me better maybe you will wonder why you ever liked such a horrible type, for no doubt I tend to gloss over my bad points in my letters and you will only learn them by being in my company.

'Oh, Happy Day' (Kuwait to Grangemouth)

From Umm-Said in Kuwait, it was plain sailing to Suez, where three more letters from Barbara were waiting.

She had been checking the laboratory results on the milk processed by Northern Dairies, learning about the different types of bacteria:

I never realised the extent to which the public are safeguarded in the purity of their milk – nor did I realise what a lot of strange things are in milk when it is first collected before being pasteurised.

John replied:

Perhaps it would be as well if you didn't describe the various milk bacteria to me, for I drink rather a lot of milk when I am at home. Nevertheless, Northern Dairies cannot regard me as a remunerative customer for I have a cousin who keeps a herd of cows and naturally we deal with them.

Barbara was keen to point out that her secretarial job involved a lot more than shorthand and typing:

Some days I hardly touch the typewriter, yet I get quite used to very sweetly persuading managers that they really do want an extra two dozen banana yoghurts, even if they do not think so. Sometimes I'm listening to a manager on the phone telling me what a shocking organisation it must be if his cream did not arrive when he wanted it, and then when he has worn himself out I point out that of course if we receive an order before it is wanted it will arrive in time. Honestly John, dealing with some of our dairy managers and area managers has given me quite an insight into the peculiarities of mankind!

Along with a photograph of John looking 'very brown' in the boat outside Venice, Barbara had received one of him in his uniform. She thought it a 'very good one, even if your cap seems to be pushed back a little'.

The now 25-year-old John explained:

I hadn't realised but it must have been taken almost five years ago, for I haven't had another one taken since then. Therefore, you will have to add a few wrinkles and lines of care, if they are to represent me now.

Barbara had been asked to help re-form the Haltemprice Young Liberals, but was doubtful about whether she would find any recruits:

There are so few people interested in Liberalism, and I have found it is more fashionable to be a Young Conservative.

John replied:

I think the majority of Liberal-minded young people have a far more independent mind than a lot of Young Conservatives and members of the Labour League of Youth, who may be quite content to follow the lead given to them by Mr Churchill (I can't get used to the 'Sir') or Mr Brown.

In her next letter, Barbara commented on the latest royal scandal to hit the headlines:

At present all the newspapers are filled with the Princess Margaret and Peter Townsend affair. As you no doubt know, it is rumoured that Peter Townsend has been exiled to Belgium out of Margaret's way. I am rather shocked at the way some of the papers are reporting on this action, one even suggests that there should be a national poll to see whether Margaret and Peter T should marry. Apart from the fact that no one knows whether or not they even want to marry, I think that it is a question that only Princess Margaret can settle, owing to the fact that she has strong religious convictions and Peter Townsend has had a divorce.

I personally am very much against divorce, especially if the marriage ceremony has taken place in a church, and although I realise that sometimes marriages can go really wrong, I think that if both partners try really hard they can pull the marriage off the rocks. I think too many people go into marriage these days with the unconscious thought that if anything goes wrong they can always get a divorce.

What John thought on the subject, we will never know, as he had already left Suez and did not receive the letter till later. While the ship was offshore at Suez, John had taken a turn on watch:

We have not much to do during anchor watches except to watch out for robbers who board the ship and try to steal our ropes, brass and other gear. Earlier during the watch, I had to chase away a fishing boat that came alongside. It was using a bonfire to attract the fish and of course in view of the very dangerous character of the oil we are carrying it wasn't safe to have it so near the ship.

It is a lovely starlit night with just the faint sliver of a new moon showing low down on the eastern horizon. The planet Venus has just risen. In fact, the setting is all set for romance. Without you sweetheart, there can be no romance for me, and I am just longing for the next occasion when on a night such as this I have you in my arms.

And that letter posted from Suez on July 14th, 1953 was the last that John sent on this trip. The next day he sent a telegram:

DUE GRANGEMOUTH 30TH HOPING FOR LEAVE TELEPHONING ON ARRIVAL ALL MY LOVE JOHN

Barbara aged 17

Barbara's family home, today

John's family home, today

John aged 17

The Mission, today

John, aged 20,
with his cap too far back.

Barbara's selfie

Barbara in her Wren uniform

John keeping cool

John (left) on the boat near Venice

Barbara sought John's opinion
on hats

John liked to see Barbara
smiling in photos

John preferred to be
photographed from the front

Barbara (right) at the caravan with
her family

CHAPTER TWO

A YEAR TO REMEMBER: JULY 1953 – AUGUST 1954

'Say You're Mine Again'

I was wondering a little what we should think of each other when we met again, but it wasn't bothering me at all for I felt confident that we were made for each other. Perhaps at that time we couldn't forecast the route the train of events would follow but I do know that all my hopes which I relished then have been accomplished. (John)

John returned to his home town of Beverley in East Yorkshire in mid-July, having been given a glowing reference by the Master of the British Surveyor:

This is to certify that Mr J.H. Witty has served as 2ⁿᵈ Officer in this vessel from 14/8/52 until present date. Whilst at sea he has had full charge of the watch from 12 am to 1pm and at no time have watches been doubled. Mr Witty has proved himself an outstandingly capable and trustworthy officer who has at all times been strictly sober, hardworking and attentive to all his duties, which he has carried out in a most praiseworthy way. In all my reports to owners I have stated that I consider him outstanding in the capable and efficient way in which he has worked, and recommended him as Chief Officer, irrespective of certificate held. Mr Witty is now leaving the vessel to prepare and sit for his Master's certificate and I wish him success in this and in the future. G. Turner, Master.

Shortly after his return, he took Barbara to meet his parents and then the couple went for a walk on Beverley Westwood. It was there that he told her for the first time that he loved her.

Do you remember our first walk on the Westwood darling, and our first picnic when your dizzy wife forgot to bring a flask? I felt very happy that day, and very proud that the most wonderful boy in the world should love me.'

On 27th August they got engaged to be married:

You know my dearest when I asked you to marry me it was the wisest thing I ever did and now we are married I am the luckiest husband alive for I don't regret anything we have done together,

They visited John's brother in Ross-on-Wye and holidayed with Barbara's sister in Norfolk. John was now busy studying for his Master's exam, but one Saturday evening in October they went to a fair in Beverley market place and enjoyed themselves on the roundabouts. In November they went to the Mission to Seamen Christmas Sale and bought a tray and loofah for the house they were buying.

'Side by Side'

After first looking at houses in Norwood in Beverley, they decided to live nearer Barbara's family in Hessle. The house they finally chose at the end of November was in Westfield Avenue, in West Hull, and they took out a ten-year mortgage of £660, paying £3-4-2 per fortnight.

Built around 1930, it was a small terraced house on a narrow road, which is now a one-way street, but there was very little traffic then. When John went back to sea, Barbara would listen out for the sound of the telegraph boy's motorbike. Today many of the front fences and walls have been removed and the gardens paved over so that cars can be parked, but back then there was a small flower garden at the front with daffodils and hyacinths, irises and roses.

As with many houses in Hull, a 'ten-foot' or back alley ran behind the houses, giving access to the back garden. This had a small lawn, an apple tree, a lilac tree, and a few fruit bushes: red and black currant, gooseberries and raspberry canes. They also found room to plant a few lettuces. At the bottom of the garden, the house still had an air-raid shelter, as did most houses at the time, with a climbing rose trained over it. Downstairs, the lounge had a bay window and an open fire. Behind it was the 'kitchenette' with a kitchen cabinet and dining table, and a small bathroom to the side. At the back of the house, a 'veranda' housed the cooker and sink, a clothes wringer and a 'copper' for heating water. A staircase led straight up from the front door. The party walls must have been quite thin as Barbara could hear whatever radio programme her neighbours were listening to and she always heard them going to bed.

On December 4th, 1954, John wrote:

Do you remember what we were doing a year ago? It was just before I went up for my Master's ticket and we were busy choosing things for our house.

He had been glad of Barbara's support:

I remember how much it cheered me up to find you waiting for me when I got off the bus in Hull on my way to the exam room.

'Eternally'

John received his certificate on the 14th December and on the 28th they got married in Hessle Church with seven bridesmaids, including their four nieces and Barbara's friends. The bridesmaids carried fur muffs to keep their hands warm, John wore his best uniform and Barbara wore a brocade dress with a high collar and pearl buttons. An article about their wedding appeared in the local newspaper, describing how they had met at the Seamen's Mission.

The following year, Barbara met an elderly lady who had been to their wedding:

It transpired that poor old Mrs Yeoman thought she was dying in church during our wedding service – apparently, she gets sudden 'attacks' – but she said she was determined not to spoil our wedding, so she sat still and hoped no one would notice, and eventually she felt better. She told mother that it was the prettiest wedding she had seen in all her life!

The couple honeymooned in Harrogate. A year later, John recalled:

It was the happiest day of my life for then my darling we became as one. At this time, we had just arrived at the Cairn Hydro and were preparing for an early night. It was rather an early night darling, but I don't think we did a lot of sleeping, did we sweetheart?

On March 12th they went to a dance, John again wearing his best uniform, the one reserved for Christmas Day and New Year's Day when he was on board ship. Later in the year, Barbara wrote:

I can hear the Gay Gordons on next door's TV. Do you remember doing it at the University Dance at the City Hall, dearest?

By the spring Barbara knew she was expecting a baby, although they did not then know that it would be a boy. They went to the theatre to see La Traviata:

It was the night we celebrated the knowledge that Patricia was on the way.

Whilst continuing his extended leave, John studied for his Extra-Masters exam and passed it with the highest mark in the country. He got his certificate on July 14th. An article about his success appeared in the Hull Daily Mail. Later he wrote to Barbara:

If it hadn't been for your encouragement and help, I don't think I should have been able to pass both exams. I am afraid we had to curtail our pleasures a bit, but I think it was worth it, don't you dearest? The occasional night out together by ourselves seemed all the better because of its rarity.

On August 6th John was appointed relieving 2nd officer while his next ship, the British Guardian, was in dry dock. They spent a month on board the ship in Falmouth. As it sailed away on August 30th, John wrote:

Thank you for making the past year the happiest year of my life. You have made me so happy dearest and I want you to remain happy whilst I am away. It can never be as nice as when we are together, but we can be happy writing to each other and looking at each other's pictures. Then we can look forward to the next time we are together – what a red-letter day that will be.

Engaged in August 1953

John proposed on Beverley Westwood

SAILOR TO WED HIS HARBOUR LIGHT

"DAILY MIRROR" REPORTER

THE girl who made four vows to be friendly—but not too friendly—with sailors, is going to marry a sailor.

A year ago Barbara Ellis, a company director's secretary, stood before the altar of the church adjoining the Flying Angel Mission for Seamen in Posterngate, Hull, and promised:

● Never to exchange telephone numbers or addresses with sailors,
● Never to meet them outside the mission,
● Never to accept invitations to ships, and
● Never to let anyone see her home after mission dances without permission.

Like thirty other "no date" girls who call themselves the Harbour Lights Guild, Barbara kept her promise.

She was helping to "keep seamen off the streets and out of moral danger," as the hard-working Rev. R. J. Barnes, the Port Chaplain, puts it.

He greets every ship into the docks and invites the crews to mission dances. "They may come with the idea of picking a girl up, but when they see there is no nonsense allowed they tell me, 'You have good girls' and like us for it."

Straight Home

Barbara danced with the seamen, smiled, talked about their families. But when the dance ended it was straight home, without escort.

But six months ago a ship's officer, John Whitty, from Beverley, Yorkshire, danced with her. They fell in love.

John told the padre. He was allowed to take her home. Now they are engaged and the wedding has been fixed for December 28.

"The seamen will miss Barbara," Miss Enid Johnson, the chaplain's secretary, told me yesterday. "She was always smiling."

"The girls must be over seventeen and attend church. After six months' probation they make their four promises before the altar and are fully enrolled."

Barbara, now twenty-four, said: "It was love at first sight."

Married in December 1953

Barbara had 7 bridesmaids

Cutting the cake

Hull dance hostess marries

From our Hull staff

A replacement is still needed by Hull's Port Chaplain, the Rev. R. J. Barnes, for his former dance hostess at the Missions to Seamen in Posterngate, Hull, 24-year-old Miss Barbara

The bride

Ellis, of Edward Street, Hessle, whose marriage to Ship's Officer John Herbert Whitty, of Beverley, took place at Hessle Parish Church yesterday

Miss Ellis and Mr. Whitty met at a dance at the Mission, and the Port Chaplain officiated at their wedding. It was the third time he had performed the marriage ceremony for former Harbour Lights, as the hostesses are known.

The house on Westfield Road, today

Outside the veranda

At the University dance

CHAPTER THREE

SEPARATED AGAIN: SEPTEMBER – DECEMBER 1954

'Smile – though your heart is aching' (Falmouth to Port de Boue)

On August 30th, 1954, John wrote:

My own dearest wife, it seems queer writing to you again, darling, knowing that I shall have to go to bed tonight by myself. Oh, how I miss you dearest and how I am hoping it will be a short trip and that we can soon be together again. No doubt you followed our progress out into the bay until we anchored. I kept looking along the cliffs with the telescope until I discovered where you were. I am sure it was you dearest, by the side of the road, with your coat hung over the fence – how I longed to be by your side.

At the same time, Barbara was writing:

After I left the docks I took my case to the station, then caught a bus intending to go into the town, but instead I got off at the beach. Afterwards I walked along the cliff tops and spent the rest of the morning watching you. I wonder if you could see me darling. I had taken my coat off because it was so hot, so my white blouse might have stood out. I hope you have a good trip to Port de Boue, dearest, and that you get there soon, because already I am looking forward to my first letter from you. Until then I shall have to be satisfied with just thinking about you all the time and remembering how happy we have been. It seems terribly empty and lonely without you darling. I feel as though part of me is missing. I hope it won't be long before we see each other again.

Barbara stood on the clifftop at Falmouth in the hot midday sun, watching the MV British Guardian leave. Then she took the overnight train back to Hull via Truro, Plymouth, Bristol and Leeds:

At Truro a gentleman helped me with my cases onto the platform, and then a porter took them across to the Bristol train and put me in a Ladies Only compartment.

She had got sunburnt whilst watching the ship sailing from Falmouth:

One arm is bright red, and I can hardly bear to touch it, but I have put some Astral on it. Wouldn't it be funny if it went brown? I should have one brown arm and one white one.

After changing trains at Bristol, the five-months pregnant Barbara was joined in the compartment by two middle-aged ladies:

They took great care of me, for I was lying down with my eyes closed when suddenly one of them wrapped my coat around me, thinking I was asleep. They said I ought to keep 'warm and out of draughts' in my condition.

At Gloucester three young army types got in this compartment. They are going home on de-mob leave. They all seem quite nice boys and told me not to move – I was taking up most of one seat.

Back home all the neighbours were talking about John being in the local papers:

Mrs Cleveland said she felt quite proud of living next to us!

The Hull Daily Mail had a picture of him in the garden, wearing his uniform and the Beverley Guardian carried the headline 'Young Beverley Man has sailed round the world five times', although the report had muddled up some of the facts. John's current path was leading towards the Port de Boue, north-west of Marseilles, via the Bay of Biscay and Gibraltar, en route to Port Said. The MV British Guardian was a new ship, first launched in April 1953. John was getting to know his fellow officers and crew:

I had quite a longish chat with the 'Old Man' on watch this afternoon and he seems very nice. The sailors seem quite a willing crowd too. 'Sparks' is quite nice too, although I can't say I agree with his views on everything. Apparently, he and his wife are the type who would rather have a car than have children. My room is looking much tidier now. That steward Godfrey is certainly a hard worker and he gave the room a good clean out this morning. In the saloon, I am sitting with 'Sparks', the Third Engineer and the Electrician. Their conversation will probably be more interesting than at the Old Man's as

I imagine the Second Engineer will monopolise the conversation there. The noisy apprentice now has the other apprentices to tell his exploits and spout his knowledge to, so he doesn't pester me.

Sharing watches, eight hours on and eight off, John watched the dolphins and sperm whales as they passed through the straits of Gibraltar:

Whilst coming round the south tip of Portugal, we saw a marvellous display of phosphorescence. As the crest of each wave broke, a blue light shone from it and made it so bright that we had no difficulty picking up the lights of other ships.

As usual he was busy changing clocks, working on the radar, the charts and the gyro:

The radar maintenance engineer in Falmouth said he couldn't get it down to an accuracy of less than 2% but I have managed to get it well below 1% this morning, so I am feeling quite pleased.

John needed to use radar to locate Port de Boue, as it was low-lying, and the weather was hazy. He also had to make especially thorough checks on the crew to make sure they weren't smoking in their beds. They pumped ballast ashore before loading Marine Diesel oil.

Lavera, where we are lying, is right at the mouth of Port de Boue harbour. Further in, a narrow canal communicates with a lake on which the rest of the refineries are situated. Just across the bay (the Gulf of Foz) is the main outlet of the River Rhone, whilst Marseilles lies to the south and east.

The oil jetty is quite a distance from the town of Port de Boue, and apart from the odd house the landscape is low and sandy with clumps of scattered grass. Dotted all around are silver oil tanks, and here and there a cluster of tall buildings glistening in the sun mark the site of a small refinery. I don't suppose I shall go ashore here, although I may go for a stroll just outside the jetty. I still have about 150 francs from the last time I was in France, but I don't suppose they will buy me much more than a haircut.

As the crew went ashore, John commented on the latest fashions:

We have a teddy boy among the apprentices. He went ashore in his stovepipe trousers in Port de Boue, though he was lacking the usual type of tie. I offered to lend him a shoelace.

Unfortunately, the crew got into trouble after visiting the nearest pub on shore:

Two of them fell out with each other and started fighting. The result was that the police turned up in strength and turfed all the crew out and back to the ship.

The Third Mate, worse for beer, missed his watch. John had given him his 150 francs to post a letter, but it couldn't be used as it was 'occupational' money and now obsolete. (This 'flag-ticket' currency, issued by the USA, was used in France following the Normandy landings in 1944. It was declared to be counterfeit by General de Gaulle when he took over the government of France following its Liberation). Fortunately, he had paid out of his own pocket, so Barbara didn't miss out after all.

'Oh Baby I get so Lonely' (Port de Boue to Mena-al-Ahmadi)

From Port-de-Boue, the British Guardian passed through the Bonifacio Strait between Corsica and Sardinia into the Tyrrhenian Sea:

The scenery on each side was quite picturesque. The chalk cliffs here look just like those near Dover and I couldn't help wishing we were homeward bound.

While John was on watch in the early hours of the morning, he saw a great array of lights stretching from one end of the horizon to the other:

As we approached closer, I could see it was a fleet of warships. There were at least three aircraft carriers in the fleet so I took it to be the American Fifth fleet, making for its base at Naples.

The sky was then lit up by an electric storm as they passed though the Straits of Messina between Italy and Sicily:

It was rather an awe-inspiring sight to see the lightning darting down amongst the mountains of Sicily. The Straits are just over a mile wide in one part, so we had a good view of both banks; the dried-up mud-filled river beds which become raging torrents when a storm bursts in the mountains; and the houses in the villages, painted delicate pastel shades, each group clustered around a white spired church. There were quite a few rowing boats in the straits, the occupants gaily waving to us as we passed.

At Port Said, John finally had his hair cut and bought two short-sleeved white shirts:

I don't like piercing the shoulders of those good sports shirts of mine for epaulettes so perhaps these will do me for a while.

They had been wearing 'whites' since entering the hotter climate. John apologised for the way his biro ink melted and ran in the heat, causing his writing to smudge. He had received two more letters from Barbara and was thinking about her life back home:

As I look at your photo on the table I can visualise you making supper or knitting and probably thinking of a ship lying in Port Said. Often when I am thinking about you I can visualise you so clearly that I am sure you must be thinking of me at that moment. Especially during the evening, I feel close to you my sweetest one. Every mile we do is one mile further from home, but I try not to think of it that way. Instead I remember that every week means one and a half days leave with you. It doesn't matter how long the trip is or how many thousands of miles we are apart you can rest assured that I am loving you and thinking about you. You have made my heart so full of happiness since we met and even when we are apart everything seems to have more meaning and purpose since I met you.

From Port Said, they continued on to Suez, where a gang of labourers caulked the seams of the wooden deck to make it watertight. As they passed through the canal and into the Red Sea, temperatures soared to 100 degrees in the shade, and the pitch started bubbling out of the deck in the heat. John was busy correcting charts, the sweat pouring off him, as the ship was invaded by swallows, hoopoes and other birds. His cabin was invaded by flies:

I am wondering whether to hunt them down before I turn in, otherwise they will hunt me down.

John's laundry had been piling up in his cabin, but it was too hot to deal with it. While Barbara was taking a hot water bottle and glass of cocoa to bed as the September nights turned colder, John was drinking '*warm chocolate treacle*' (a bar of Dairy Milk chocolate that had melted in his jacket pocket, but mercifully stayed in its wrapper). He was worried about how the new Junior Engineer would stand the heat '*for it appears he doesn't sweat and even this spell of warm weather has made him a bit groggy*'.

It was a relief to leave the Red Sea and head towards the Persian Gulf, but the heat was replaced by other hazards:

At first the sun didn't come out from behind clouds, then the horizon went hazy and finally thick fog descended upon us. Most of the day was spent trying to find the ship's position as we groped our way through the fog with the whistle going every couple of minutes.

Meanwhile, it was the electrician's 21st birthday so John covered a key with silver paper and gave it to him. Then they had a celebration:

It was quite a nice get-together, although for a good part of the evening the Tynesiders and the Scotchmen were busy arguing about the relative merits of their two districts.

'Little Things Mean a Lot' (Mena-al Ahmadi

Arriving at Mena-al-Ahmadi, John was delighted to get five letters from Barbara:

When at last I saw a small boat coming out to the ship, I was the first to the pilot's ladder to help get the mail on board.

Now that they had set up home together, John and Barbara's letters often deal with domestic issues. No longer working at Northern Dairies, Barbara felt she must account for her expenditure from her monthly housekeeping budget of £15:

I was rather worried as to where it had gone until I checked my spending list and found that apart from food, everyday expenses and material for baby clothes etc, I had spent £2-12-6 on coal, £1-0-0 on a passport and £1-16-0 on photographs.

She also found it necessary to apologise:

I am afraid your careless wife laddered another pair of nylons today, so I have got some more to replace them.

While John was sweltering in the Middle East, Barbara needed to light the fire, a job which John had done when he was at home. She decided that she needed to get a fire scuttle as she didn't like going out in the dark for coal. John agreed:

It certainly will be a good idea to get a coal scuttle as we shall need one before winter sets in. You seem to be managing very well about the house however and seem to have got the knack of making fires all right.

He suggests that she ask his father's advice on the small holes which had appeared in their dresser and were most probably woodworm. Since John came on leave in July 1953, Barbara had got to know her in-laws well and regularly visited them in Beverley. Sometimes she would spend a weekend with them:

I had my hot water bottle wrapped in your green striped pyjama jacket, darling, the one you wore(?) when we slept there at Easter. So, I cuddled the bottle and pretended it was you.

John's parents told her about John as a baby and little boy:

Apparently, you were a most precise little boy. She said you once told Ken (John's brother) that there was only 'black or white – no grey – it was either the truth or a fib'. I could just imagine you saying it darling.

Sometimes the conversation with John's parents moved on to current affairs. Haile Selassie was back in power as the Emperor of Ethiopia after his wartime exile in England. He was hailed by Rastafarians as the new Messiah:

We sat a long time over tea, and the conversation went from churches to religion, then to the Emperor of Ethiopia. It is claimed that he is a descendant of the son of Solomon and the Queen of Sheba. Mother remarked that she did not know the Queen of Sheba had taken a son back with her, whereupon Dad informed us that perhaps she had gone back too soon to tell!

We had quite a lazy evening, just talking and reading in front of a big fire. I do miss you though darling at such times, for I keep thinking of other evenings we have spent like that when you and I shared the settee. Before I left, my foot went through the hall floor, near the front door. It has been very weak there for some time, and Dad was hoping the rent man would go through it!

While John's mother sewed and knitted, his father was making a rug to go in front of John and Barbara's fireplace. Barbara also had the help of her own parents, who lived not far away in Hessle. Her father came round to cut the grass which had grown a foot high whilst Barbara and John had been on board ship in Falmouth. He had brought his clippers but then borrowed a lawn-mower from a neighbour. This neighbour also had a telephone, unlike John and Barbara, so would sometimes take calls from Barbara's mother if she needed to make urgent contact. Barbara would regularly join her mother on shopping trips into town, coffee mornings and visits to relatives.

Her mornings however were spent doing housework. In those days before vacuum-cleaners, most floors were covered with lino, with perhaps a square of carpet:

> I got up about 7.30 this morning and after breakfast I dusted and mopped round the bedroom, swept and dusted the staircase, cleaned out the fireplace, swept the lounge carpet and dusted, then swept the dining room and veranda, and finished off by washing the bathroom and veranda floors.

Then there were the outside jobs to be done:

> I washed all the outside paintwork of the lower windows and door and porch front way. I used the steps so that I did not have to reach up, but the wind was blowing, and I had difficulty in keeping my skirt down – it was a good job there weren't any men around! I also cleaned the step and swilled the front and it all looked very nice, but after all the rain today it will look no better.

One day she suffered another wardrobe malfunction:

> Yesterday morning when I went out I lost a suspender. I had no idea where I lost it and only hoped no one was walking behind me when it dropped! This morning when I went out I saw a suspender in the middle of Sunbeam Road and I presumed it was mine but didn't stop to pick it up.

Presumably, Barbara was appropriately dressed when she met the Lady Mayoress who had been visiting the Seamen's Mission. She had asked to be introduced to Barbara, having read the newspaper articles about their marriage the previous year:

> After being introduced, she said, 'I can understand why he fell in love with you' and 'You certainly do look very happy.'

As well as possessing a lawn mower and a telephone, Barbara's neighbour had just acquired a television set:

> It was fitted yesterday, and this morning she called me in to see it. It is a very nice set and fitted ready for commercial TV. Mrs Cleveland said I can go in anytime I wish to see it.

Like Barbara's brother, also called John, Mr Cleveland worked on the trawlers, and a good trip would give the opportunity to splash out when they got home. Locally the trawlermen were known as 'three-day millionaires' as they would spend their earnings in the few days between their hazardous trips to the fishing grounds. It would be years before Barbara and John got a television, but the radio was a constant companion:

> *I am dependent on it for the correct time, apart from it being good company when I am on my own.*

When it stopped working she paid the alarming sum of £1-15-0 to have it working again. She then had a surprise:

> *I thought you were on your way to South America, but I just heard on the wireless that you have for the last fifteen minutes been presenting the programme 'Anything Goes'! I think it must be someone who just shares your name, for the voice was not nearly so nice as yours, darling.*

'Three Coins in the Fountain'

Occasional trips to the cinema and theatre provided additional entertainment. Barbara and her mother went to see the film 'Three coins in the Fountain' at the Plaza:

> *It was very good, particularly the scenery of Rome and Venice. One scene was exactly the same as on my musical box. (A present from John)*

They also saw the play 'The Four-Poster':

> *The whole play is centred round a four-poster bed and covers thirty-five years. It begins on the wedding night of the young couple and ends the day they sell the bed. I was particularly amused by the second scene, where the young wife is expecting a baby, and the husband has labour pains! I wonder if you will get labour pains darling. If you get sharp shooting pains spreading from the small of your back to your tummy, you will know our Patricia, or Michael, is about to make an appearance.*

John was certainly thinking about Barbara and the baby she was carrying, keeping a list of baby's things 'so that I can visualise what (s)he is wearing when I am not at home'.

Meanwhile, Barbara was busy embroidering pillow cases with butterflies and flowers, making small nappies out of a roll of white lint, knitting vests and sewing matinee coats. She had used seven yards of ribbon to trim baby clothes.

Don't do too much darling, advised John, *and overwork yourself, for we can always buy any baby things which you haven't had time to make.*

John had been reading a ship's captain's medical guide to childbirth and was reassured by what Barbara told him about the nursing home she had booked:

The matron assured me that they do not believe in the mother having a lot of pain, and always give something to ease it and bring the baby more quickly.

At the end of every letter John now sent love and kisses to Patricia or 'Micheal' John. (Barbara would correct his misspelling later). Barbara wondered whether they would need both names:

I seem to be getting fatter every day, especially at the back. I think we are having twins darling, one at the back and one at the front.

'No one but You" (Mena-al-Ahmadi to Eva Peron)

The British Guardian was taking the cargo loaded at Mena round the Cape of Good Hope and across to South America, arriving about four weeks later to discharge at Eva Peron and San Lorenzo, a small port lying 250 miles up the River Plate. From there they would take on water and bunkers at Montevideo in Uruguay. He did not relish the long wait between letters:

Five or six days seem a long time to wait between letters. I don't know how I shall do when there are three or four weeks between ports. I shall just have to get some of your old letters and re-read them.

John was hopeful that they would make just the one run to South America, in which case he might visit a UK port before Christmas, but it was possible that they would do three runs from Mena to Eva Peron, which would take a full nine months. With the baby due in December, he must have been afraid of completely missing his or her first six months:

At one time British Tanker Company didn't like you taking leave at intervals of less than one year, but now I believe they encourage you taking leave after nine months so next June should be the time for my next long leave.

Not surprisingly he was starting to think about possible shore jobs. He wondered about doing a BSc correspondence course in Naval Architecture but ruled it out for financial reasons. He considered a career in cargo-surveying or even teaching:

I think teaching is quite a comfortable job, providing you can make ends meet. To become a surveyor, it seems I should have to spend a good few more years at sea – away from you my darling – and I want to be as little away from you as possible. To start teaching off on the right step, I should need my teaching diploma. I think it takes about nine months, but the maximum grant would be about £50 a term.

The British Guardian left Mena el Ahmadi at the end of September after loading cargo and sailed towards the Cape of Good Hope via the Mozambique channel between Madagascar and Africa. While Barbara was marking his route on the atlas he had left for her, John was enjoying the sun on 'Monkey Island', the top deck of the ship, drinking lime juice and appreciating the fact that he would receive the Eastern Bonus from Port Said until they rounded the Cape of Good Hope. He was also enjoying an improvement in the food:

The tea tonight was very nice, and I wish you could have been here to sample it. First, we had scrambled egg, then fresh salmon and mayonnaise, followed by cold meat and salad, with peaches and cream as the sweet.

Back home however there was a dock strike which created a shortage of Danish eggs. Barbara complained:

I had to pay 6½d each for English eggs. Isn't it a terrible price!

She had been making a sweet for tea:

I sliced some oranges and then made an orange jelly, whipped in some evaporated milk, stirred in the oranges and left it to set. I wonder if it would have met with your approval, darling. It seems ages since I prepared a meal for you, doesn't it?

The British Surveyor crossed the equator, so John was looking forward to seeing the Southern Cross and other unfamiliar stars when he was on Middle Watch during the night:

However, I shall watch the northern stars more and dreamily wonder whether you too are watching them.

As navigator, John was using his sextant to take altitudes, but his readings differed from those taken by the Captain and Third Mate:

Now we always agree to differ by one minute and take the mean, as none of us will admit our sextants are out.

He complained that the Captain didn't seem to have enough work to do and interfered unnecessarily. In John's spare time, he was reading a book which was trying to reconcile scientific theories to current religious thought. One of the ideas that it considered was the extent to which human lives follow a preordained pattern. John concluded:

Although the individual has a choice of paths, the path of the world and of mankind in general can still be predicted.

The path of the British Guardian headed south. As they rounded the Cape, the weather changed. For a week there was no sign of land or ships. An albatross joined them:

Some of these birds have a wingspan of 14 feet, and it gives you quite a start when one of them glides by you during the night.

They changed back into their 'blues,' of battledress jacket and flannels, and put the heating on as they entered the South Atlantic. As the ship noisily creaked and rolled in the gales, John had to wear a monsoon coat and sea boots. In the meantime, Barbara was struggling again with the fire:

After three attempts it really seemed to be burning, so I popped out to the shops and phoned mother. When I came back, instead of seeing a nice fire, all I saw was lots of coal piled up. For the next three quarters of an hour I tussled with it, using firelighters, paper, matches, sugar, and eventually it condescended to go.

Once the fire was blazing away, it heated the hot water and it was a shame to waste it. Barbara's mother had been to tea and to spend the evening with her, knitting for the baby:

As my water was very hot I asked Mother if she would like a bath, so she had one before supper. The water is now quite hot again, so I think I shall have one before I go to bed. Coke is definitely far better than coal for heating the water.

Barbara was also busy making clothes for the baby, now knitting vest no. 4, embroidering matinee coat no.4 and adding ribbons to nighty no.4 for the baby. He or she was making their presence felt:

A minute ago, I was writing with one hand on my tummy, when suddenly a small hand or foot pushed me, and I was able to hold it for a second. As I watch my tummy I can see it moving and being poked out first in one place and then in another.

Barbara did not however limit herself to preparing for the baby. She was also investigating alternative career options on John's behalf. She went to Friary Chambers in Hull to see Mr Upton of the Navigators and Engineering Officers' Union. He described John as 'a damned brainy chap who deserves to go places.'

The place John was heading for at the moment was Eva Peron in Argentina. This was the name given between 1952 and 1955 to La Plata, the capital city of Buenos Aires Province. Also known as Evita, Eva Peron was the First Lady of Argentina and had been given the title 'Spiritual Leader of the Nation' before her death in 1952. Her story was brought to a more modern audience in the musical 'Evita', starring Madonna in the film version. At Eva Peron, John found eleven letters from Barbara, together with large coloured photographs taken in Falmouth. He sent off the batch of letters that he had written during the voyage from Mena and started a new letter, describing his surroundings:

The town of Eva Peron is actually a few miles from the port but as there is quite a decent sized town at the port we didn't bother going all the way into Eva Peron. The town is mainly composed of corrugated iron dwellings but some of them have been made to look nice. The more substantial houses are brick-built and faced with cement. Most of them are painted cream or white and have very attractive flower gardens. On the other hand, only the main streets are paved, the rest being merely mud or gravel tracks with open drains running along each side. The country is very low-lying and is criss-crossed with streams and swamps. Thus, there are any amount of insects abounding, as well as frogs, water-rats and other reptiles.

Most families seem to keep a few fowl, and these are free to wander about the streets. Also, in the streets, wandering around, are the gaucho's horses. They seem to ride into town on them and then leave them wandering around while they attend to their business.

He had reluctantly been persuaded to join the Mate and a group of engineers in a tour of Swift's meat factory:

It certainly gave you an insight into what happened before the meat finally found its way onto the table in the form of corned beef. I should have liked to see the canning factory, but the guide spoke no English and seemed far more eager to show us the abattoirs. One had to look at the whole process objectively, otherwise one could quite easily have been sick.

The crew meanwhile had been fishing for catfish:

They boil off the flesh and the bone is said to resemble a crucifix. The resemblance didn't live up to my expectations.

For once, the sailors were relatively well behaved on shore:

We have not had much trouble with the crew here, although most of them have been tight at some time or another. The night before last, two of the firemen landed up in jail, whilst the same night one of the ABs staggering back fell over a low bridge. Two of the catering staff thought they had missed the ferry, so they came across in a rowing boat they had found. I heard these two singing away and eventually made out the boat's shape as it zigzagged crazily across the river. They will now have to do without beer for another two months or more, hence why they must make the most of the opportunity.

'There must be a reason' (Argentina to Persian Gulf)

From Eva Peron, they sailed to Montevideo in Uruguay for water and bunkers (fuel):

The town of Montevideo looked very impressive with quite a number of fine buildings and not so much of the dilapidated look which characterizes such a lot of these South American towns. However, we were not to see it at closer quarters for soon the bunkering and water barges were alongside.

November brought the long journey back across the South Atlantic, round the Cape of Good Hope and up to the Persian Gulf. There they would follow the Khur Musa river to Bandar Mashur to discharge ballast and load cargo. The rough weather in the South Atlantic played havoc with John's task of correcting charts:

The ship made a particularly heavy roll and the next moment the red ink was sliding off the chart room table onto the floor. Of course, I made a dive for it, but I was just too late to stop it spilling. At this very moment the ship rolled the other way and the violet ink went hurtling off in the other direction leaving a smear of violet on the chart.

When he wasn't correcting charts, working on the radar or gyro, John was teaching the apprentices. He decided to spend his spare time reading the Bible right the way through, with a dictionary by his side, even neglecting his laundry to finish it:

Most of what we know of the Bible seems to me to have been taught us as children, yet quite a lot of what we know of the Bible is hardly suitable for children to read and needs an adult mind to appreciate it. Apart from its teachings, the Bible gives you an insight into the way the people of biblical times lived, and as such I find it most interesting.

After reading the Old Testament, he broke off from reading the Bible to read 'The Snow Goose' by Paul Gallico:

It was a most moving and interesting little tale about a lonely man who loved birds but lacked the love of his fellow beings.

Then he continued with the New Testament, which left him with mixed feelings:

The religion of the church today seems very similar to that preached by Paul, but I wonder whether it shouldn't have advanced as it did no doubt during Biblical times. The High Priest of the Jews tried to keep religion the same as it was in the time of Moses and were proved to be in error by Christ. I suppose it is one fault of an established church that it cannot easily retract any of its teachings.

The crew meanwhile were keeping themselves busy making sailing ships and putting them in bottles, taught by 'Chippy'. They were also making toy electric trams and ships. At the beginning of November, Barbara received the letters John had sent from Eva Peron. She hoped that he might be heading homewards after the Persian Gulf:

If you were to come home now I should travel to wherever you are and neither of our mothers could stop me (they would both try). I would risk the baby being born at sea. You could always deliver it.

She sent John a telegram to say that she had received his letters. John had devised a code to use when sending telegrams to Barbara in order to reduce the cost. This would enable him to give dates and names of ports. He suggested it could also be used to convey information about illnesses:

MA= person indicated has illness, followed by a letter of the alphabet indicating the nature of the illness e.g. MA(A) = measles, MA(B) = influenza.

The code WAWCH which would end most of their telegrams meant 'All my love and kisses, my darling. All well'. Barbara was impressed with the code and planned to use it, with one exception:

I think I will still send the one about the baby's birth in full, just to make sure you get the right information.

Barbara had arranged to have a 'Luxi-car' taxi to take her to the nursing home on 'D-Day':

The manager said no matter what time of the day or night, they will have one out in a few minutes, so long as I say it is a maternity case.

For the time being, the only communication they could have was by telegram. There had been no opportunity to collect mail since leaving Argentina, but they continued to write to each other on a daily basis, sharing the minutiae of their lives, and assuring each other of their love. As December approached, John thought increasingly about parenthood:

I think most of the trouble in child guidance is giving the child sufficient love and attention without spoiling it, and I know that you will do just that. In fact, we shall both love Baby very much and whether it is a boy or a girl won't make an ounce of difference to our love for him or her.

He hoped to receive letters at Bandar Mashur, but the mail had gone astray so he had to leave empty-handed and without further news until reaching Suez.

'Rain, Rain, Rain' (Persian Gulf to Suez)

Bandar Mashur, John wrote, *is rather at the back of beyond, the nearest town being Bandar Shahpur. Between Bandar Shahpur and our berth, the country mainly consists of mud-flats with occasional bits of harder ground where a little vegetation grows. There were quite a lot of different birds flying about and feeding on the mud-flats, including quite a number of storks. I wondered whether one of the storks was on its way to England to visit a certain house in Westfield Road.*

When the ship received orders for Land's End, John desperately hoped they might head for a UK port so that he could try for even an hour or two of unofficial leave. He sent Barbara a telegram and she was delighted with the news:

What a lovely surprise it was this morning to receive your telegram. I had not expected hearing quite so soon, and I was thrilled to know that when you leave the Persian Gulf you are coming in this direction.

But the ship headed instead towards Antwerp for engine repairs:

I am so sorry we are not coming to an English port next for I did so want to see you. However, that is the sort of thing that happens in this job. It will at least be something to be able to speak to you on the phone.

Their journey to Suez was delayed slightly by a heavy thunderstorm, with hailstones measuring up to an inch in diameter. The hail was so dense that the ship had to anchor until it passed. Once they were back in warmer climes, John again enjoyed the sun on 'Monkey Island', but was darning socks ready for colder weather:

It should be quite a pleasant trip as far as the Mediterranean. Apparently, you are having a number of gales round the UK coast, but it doesn't matter what gales or bad weather you are having, I should rather be round the UK than out here.

While John sunned himself, Barbara was indeed enduring cold rain, sleet and frost. There were serious floods in Hull, with between one and two feet of water in the streets at high tide:

Someone caught a fish on Whitefriargate!

'This Ole House'

Barbara managed to keep the fire going for several days, only mending it occasionally. With that nest-making instinct that often besets mothers-to-be, she was busy decorating the dining room. She had no difficulty in stripping off the old wallpaper border, but she found the painting somewhat challenging:

Although the windows and skirtings do not look too bad for an amateur, I am afraid the doors do not look good at all, and I wish I had left them alone. Still, the damage is done now, so we shall just not have to look at them.

Her father came round to hang the wallpaper, which must have been a relief, but Barbara still had to scrub the floor, re-lay the carpet, wash and re-hang the curtains, then wash-leather the furniture and windows. And it wasn't only the dining room that got revamped in readiness for the baby:

I bought a new dishcloth, as the one we have been using all our married life has finally become too threadbare for use. I have had to disentangle it from the plug-hole after every washing up.

John was also thinking about the house:

Next time I am home we shall have to go out and choose wallpaper and furnishings for Baby's room. It is nice though shopping for our own home and it will be fun preparing a little room for Baby to go into when he/she is a bit older.

'Let's Get Together' (Suez to Antwerp)

At Suez in early December, John received five letters from Barbara, the first he had received since they had left Argentina. There was still no sign of the ones that had gone astray. He discovered that Barbara was going to move in with her mother, sharing her bed, until the baby was born. She was concerned as to whether their house was insured in case of a break-in during her absence. All the sewing and shopping was done ready for the baby, except for a few outstanding items:

A dozen more nappies, lace for the christening gown and material for two more dresses. I am going to make the under-dress of the christening gown out of the white maternity slip I started to make for myself but never finished.

She was hoping the baby clothes would soon be needed:

I hope Baby does not go a long time after 9th December before putting in an appearance, and I am sure you will be waiting desperately for the telegram telling you that our son or daughter has arrived safely.

John was also ready and waiting. On December 7th he wrote:

'Sparks' is already on his toes for the message. This afternoon there was a message for the ship and I was waiting outside the radio room door in case it was from you. I do hope Baby has been born before we reach Antwerp, then you will perhaps be able to send me a nice long letter telling me all about him/

her. I shall want to know everything about him – what colour eyes – what colour his hair (if any) – how often he cries and all the other little things which will help me to visualise her/him until you get a photograph taken.

Little did either of them know what a long wait it would be. Certainly, the baby was very active:

Talking about Baby, she or he has having its evening constitutional, and it is very obvious as it moves from one side to another. I do not know where the head is, but there seems to be a surfeit of arms and legs. I trust it has a head and is not just a mass of limbs!

The British Guardian had now passed through Suez and back into the Mediterranean, so they were again wearing their 'blues' in the colder weather. There were strong winds and rainy squalls until they skirted the coast of Tunisia and passed through the Straits of Gibraltar, heading northwards towards England '*only to let it slip by on our Port side as we push our way up the Channel.*' John was hoping that it wouldn't be too long before Barbara could visit the ship:

I was wondering the other day what countries you have your passport endorsed for. It would be as well to get it endorsed for all the Northern European countries. Then that would make it simpler to get a Visa.

He then added:

I don't suppose you would be able to come across to the continent until after Baby is weaned, but perhaps you may be able to give me a better idea of this. In any case I think it would be wise to enquire from the doctor the wisdom of travelling with Baby. You would have to particularly careful if you were feeding Baby for you wouldn't have to do anything that might stop Baby's breakfast.

Fog delayed their arrival in Antwerp, but they eventually berthed on December 19th:

As we were making fast alongside the jetty, we saw a man staggering across to the ship with two mail bags, and soon willing hands were helping him to get them aboard. Even so I was hardly prepared for the multitude of letters which were waiting for me in my cabin. No less than 21 letters from you darling.

Barbara's letters had been sent between October 5th and December 14th so John was finally able to catch up. He was however interrupted by needing to attend to the ballast:

> It should have been my evening off but as today is the Third Mate's birthday I told him he could go ashore. He has just arrived back, none the worse for the celebrations, which is more than I can say for some of the sailors.

John gave his approval to the Christmas presents that Barbara had bought for his family and thanked her for reminding him that 'Michael' is spelt AE and not EA. It was now ten days after the expected date for Michael or Patricia's arrival:

> Several times a day I get asked whether I have heard any more news. Sometimes it is the Captain, sometimes a sailor and sometimes the cabin boy. I don't know how they all got to know about our expected offspring.

For Barbara, life at her mother's was a lot noisier than in her own home, especially when her youngest brother, Donald, was home on leave, and her brother John and his wife visited with their two children:

> I have never found letter-writing so difficult. Every few words I have to knock off writing to answer a question or to play with one of the kiddies.

Donald was fascinated by the sight of his heavily pregnant sister:

> He must have said a dozen times or more – 'Well, I should never have thought you could have altered so much,' and 'What has happened to my slim little sister?'

Other people remarked however on how well and pretty she looked:

> I shall soon be swelling in other places than my tummy with all the compliments I have been receiving lately.

She was still feeling fit and active, but there was no sign of Baby arriving, despite Barbara taking regular doses of castor oil. She asked her doctor if she could fly over to Antwerp to join John, but 'he said very definitely not.'

She confessed to some extravagant spending:

> I am afraid I have been rash again darling and bought a little milk pan. I have no conscience about this, as we definitely needed a pan for boiling milk

only, before Baby comes. Even if I breastfeed him or her, as I want to, there may be occasions when it is necessary to heat milk.

On the date the British Guardian was due to arrive in Antwerp, Barbara waited impatiently for a phone call, not knowing about the delay:

My theme song today is 'Ring, telephone, ring'. All yesterday and today we have had the doors open and the wireless subdued, and everyone has been listening for the phone.

When he was finally able to ring her from the office by the gate of the refinery, the line wasn't very clear, and she couldn't hear everything John said. He also found it less than ideal:

There is no privacy and sometimes it is a job hearing with all the other people in the room.

However, he was able to send her flowers while they were in port. On December 22ⁿᵈ the British Surveyor set sail from Antwerp. Barbara was distraught when she missed his last call:

All day I have been thinking about you, and wondering if you had sailed, and then to miss your phone-call was the last straw.

John hoped that he wouldn't be away much longer:

A nice trip to Syria or the Lebanon and then home would suit me.

John was doing all the night watches so that he could have the maximum time off should they call at a UK port afterwards. Meanwhile they each prepared for spending apart their first Christmas as a married couple. Barbara was pleasantly surprised to receive a tax refund, which was £5 more than she had expected:

I thought you would not mind if, out of the extra, I bought a blouse for Christmas, as I am beginning to feel rather dowdy in the same old maternity things. I certainly did not expect to be wearing maternity clothes for Christmas. The price was rather more than I intended, £2-16-0, but it should wear well, and after all the Income Tax people are paying for it.

'Let's have another Party'

On Christmas Eve, Barbara did some last-minute shopping and put the finishing touches to outfits that she had been making for her nieces:

> By the time we had finished all our work, and had supper, it was nearly midnight, so we sorted out all the Christmas presents, then after midnight we opened them.

Presents for John and Barbara included a set of soup spoons, a tray cloth and a tea-pot stand. Despite their late night, Barbara and her parents got up early on Christmas Day to attend the 7.30 Holy Communion Service at church. When they got home, she helped her mother with the housework and cooking the dinner. After they had washed up, they settled down to listen to the Queen's speech. More relations came for tea and stayed into the evening:

> After the kiddies went to bed, we spent the rest of the evening eating fruit, sweets, nuts etc, and played one or two games. At nine o'clock we drank a toast to our absent loved ones and had some Christmas cake.

There was not much celebrating on board the British Guardian on Christmas Eve, apart from a gin and some cream biscuits in the apprentice's cabin, but Christmas Day started at 10.30 am with whisky in the Mate's cabin, followed by drinks with the Captain. After a couple of beers, John relieved the Third Mate on the bridge so that he could join the party:

> The Third Mate came up again shortly and I went down to partake of the dinner – soup, fish, turkey, pork, Christmas pudding – and I enjoyed myself wading through the various courses. However, when I returned to the bridge the poor old Third Mate was just beginning to feel the after-effects of the whisky he had been drinking and he looked as white as a sheet. He managed to reach his cabin, whereupon he flopped down on his settee and did not wake again until nearly teatime. Anyhow the tea was very nice (even though most of the stewards were incapable of serving it) so the Third Mate was able to make up for the dinner he missed. After tea a number of us gathered in the Sixth Engineer's cabin where we had some more beers and had a good sing-song. I finally turned in just after 9pm but of course was up again at midnight. I noticed the Old Man was up on the bridge at midnight and I wondered if he was staying up to see if I was sober. However, he must have been quite satisfied for he turned in soon after.

December 28th was their wedding anniversary. Barbara wrote:

> *I do not think I shall ever forget that day which marked the beginning of so very much happiness.*

She sent John a telegram and for a moment he thought Baby had arrived, but there was no sign yet of '*little lazybones*'. He busied himself with correcting charts and completing the end of year inventories. On December 30th, Barbara had a check-up at the nursing home:

> *When I went to be examined, as I snuggled under the blankets I found something hot, and on investigating found it to be a hot water bottle. I thought it was very thoughtful of them to have put it in. Dr Moorhouse also very thoughtfully warmed his stethoscope and various instruments before he placed them on me. He said it is almost certain that we have been a month out in our reckoning and that Baby will be due between 5th and 9th January. He said that I am perfectly fit, and that Baby is strong, although not exceptionally big. (I thought Baby must be a miniature giant by the size I feel).*

John of course did not receive this letter for some time. December 31st brought him some bad news. He wrote:

> *Today is the last day of 1954 but I am afraid the news I have to usher in the New Year isn't so good. Last night we received our orders and we are bound once more to Bandar Mashur to load another cargo of crude oil. This time we are taking it to the new refinery at Kwinana, just south of Fremantle in Western Australia. This means no possibility of coming home before March, unless the orders are changed.*

Fortunately, Barbara was as yet unaware of this setback. Her trawlerman brother John had just been on an exceptionally good fishing trip:

> *They did quite well on the market today and John had a good 'pick-up' so I can see Joyce will get her beaver lamb fur coat, or they will get a television set, or something else very big.*

They would be taking the children to the pantomime on New Year's Eve, and Barbara agreed to babysit for them in the evening so that they could go out and celebrate in style before he sailed again the next day. On January 1st, 1955, John wrote:

A Happy New Year Darling. I wonder what you are doing today my sweetheart. There was quite a party in my cabin last night after I opened my case of beer. The Third Mate, Mate, Chief Steward, Sixth Engineer and Third Engineer all came in to drink to the New Year. Several of them had brought in fresh stocks of beer so at midnight I had had all the beer that was good for me. Of course, at midnight we rang the traditional sixteen bells, blew the whistle, rang the telegraph and made as much noise as possible. Later those off watch went into the Old Man's cabin for some more drinks whilst I walked up and down the wings of the bridge, keeping a lookout and incidentally trying to keep myself awake. About half past two I made the mistake of sitting down on the chart room settee for a minute and my head was just beginning to nod when I heard the Old Man coming up the ladder. That rallied my dulling senses together and by 3 am I had overcome the feeling of tiredness.

Barbara had also been trying to stay awake on New Year's Eve. She was hoping her brother and his wife wouldn't be too late back as she was feeling sleepy. She had read in that evening's newspaper that the Suez Canal was closed for at least eight days, due to a steel railway bridge falling on the oil tanker 'World Peace,' and it was estimated that 300 ships would be affected. She wondered whether it would mean a long hold-up for the British Guardian or whether they would go round by the Cape of Good Hope to the Middle East.

On New Year's Day, John received the much hoped for change of orders. The radio message informed them that they were to proceed to the port of Tripoli in the Lebanon to load crude oil, and then to Land's End for Orders. Although this could mean they would be redirected to any refinery in Northern Europe, there was a chance that it could be a UK port. He wrote:

If it is a port on the near continent I hope to be able to phone you, and if it is in the UK I shall try to get home if it is at all possible.

Early on January 2nd Barbara wrote:

Just before 5 am this morning I started with niggly pains in my back and tummy and they have continued until now, 7.25, so I am hoping this is it.

John however had not heard from Barbara since receiving the telegram on their wedding anniversary. He wrote the next day:

I wonder if today will bring the long-awaited telegram, for tomorrow 'Sparks' will be closed down as we shall be in a port. It seems such a long time I have been waiting to hear news of Baby's arrival and no doubt it will have seemed twice as long to you.

On January 4th, he received a telegram:

MICHAEL JOHN 8LB ARRIVED 11/30 3RD WAWCH = BARBARA

CHAPTER FOUR

FIRST BORN: JANUARY 1955 – SEPTEMBER 1955

'My Son, My Son' (Tripoli to Finnart)

Hello! My Dearest One. Thank you very much my dearest one for the telegram I received from you last night, heralding Baby's arrival. I do hope you had a not too difficult time during the birth period and that you are now beginning to feel better again. Baby must have been born just before we arrived at Tripoli and whilst I was finishing off my letter to you.

The good news soon spread:

This morning practically everybody on the ship has been congratulating me, and the Old Man gave me a bottle of whisky a few minutes ago, so that we can drink to Michael John and his future. People have kept telling me it would be a boy, but I had quite an open mind about it. However now that he is born I am glad that Baby is a boy, and then perhaps later on we can have a girl.

I also bought a crate of beer and entertained several of the officers in my cabin during the morning, but in the evening all the rest of them came into my cabin to drink to Michael John's health and to wish you and Baby well.

In the nursing home, Barbara received a bouquet of flowers from John:

The carnations and daffodils are on my locker, and the others are on the chimney piece, so I see your flowers whichever way I turn my head.

She would have to content herself with looking at flowers, as her baby was only brought to her for feeding. The rest of the time he remained with the other babies in the nursery. However, the feeding had started well, with Michael starting to gain weight almost immediately. As for Barbara:

I have a bust-line which can beat Marilyn Monroe's!

That may have been more to John's liking than the details that followed:

Dr Moorhouse came to see me this morning and seemed pleased with my progress. He looked at my stitches and said that they come out tomorrow morning, as the flesh had healed. However, Sister said I might as well have a more comfortable night tonight and that she would take them out this evening. She first of all warned me that they would hurt as Dr Moorhouse always stitched tight and stitched deep. I was glad of the warning, for it really did hurt, but I bit my thumb and thought of you, and it was not too bad, but I was in a cold sweat when she finished. Sister showed me the length of the stitches – two were 2½ inches and two were almost 3 inches – no wonder I could not sit up! Afterwards Sister gave me a blanket bath, then I sat on a chair whilst the nurse made my bed. It did seem funny to put my legs out of bed, and I was glad to sit down.

Barbara had no recollection of the stitches being put in as she was under chloroform when her baby was delivered and had to wait several hours for its effects to wear off before she could see him. It was now five days after the birth, but Barbara still only saw Michael when a feed was scheduled:

After feeding him I usually snuggle him down for a few minutes before he is taken to the nursery, and he moves his little legs until he finds me, then puts his feet on me. Also, when I am feeding him, if he can get a hand free he puts it on me and already he has a very tight grasp. This morning when he came in for his 10 am feed, his hair was quite wavy after being washed so I pushed it into little curls at the top, and it looked very sweet.

I am afraid Michael will be a bit spoilt and expect a lot of cuddling when he gets home, for we always have our babies for quarter of an hour or more after we have fed them. I am told that it is not like this in the maternity hospital. As soon as they have finished feeding there, they are snatched away until the next feed.

A stay of ten days in the nursing home was normal. Barbara described her daily schedule:

5.30 cup of tea
6.00 baby's feed

6.30 wash etc

8.00 breakfast

10.00 feeding time

10.30 cocoa

12.00 lunch

2.00 feeding time

3.00-4.15 visitors

4.15 tea

5.15 wash etc

6.00 feeding time

7.00-8.30 visitors

8.30 supper

9.30 feeding time

10.00 lights out

A week after giving birth, Barbara was allowed to get up:

We sat in our dressing gowns by the fire knitting, talking and listening to the wireless, and we had quite a pleasant morning, though we had to move when the maid came to hoover the room, so we curled up on our beds. Last night, just before feeding time, Night Sister flew in and said, 'Are you two up?' We assured her we were, so she asked us if we would help giving babies out. We both shot out of bed and into our dressing gowns and slippers, for that was the request we had been waiting for but did not expect it until today. This morning Sister asked me if I would go along to watch the babies being bathed. I learnt that our son screams when he is being soaped but enjoys having water splashed over him. He certainly can shout when he wants to. Sister said he is not a 'quiet little thing like his mother'.

On the tenth day, Barbara was allowed a bath herself and was looking forward to getting dressed and going home in a couple of days. She and her room-mate were moved into what Matron described as the 'state room':

It is the big drawing room downstairs, and we have divan beds at either side of the fireplace, so my last night here is being spent in quite luxurious surroundings.

How Barbara had envied her room-mate and the other new mothers who had received visits from their husbands! However, she received some news to cheer her up. John sent her two telegrams. The first said that the ship would be coming to Finnart, on the west coast of Scotland, on January 15th. Barbara hoped that he might be able to visit her, even if it was only for a few hours:

I just refuse to think of the possibility of you coming so near and not being able to see me, and our Michael. I got your telegram just before Michael came in for his 10 am feed, and I felt so happy that when he came in, I gave him an extra big hug and a kiss and told him his Daddy is coming home. I am afraid your son's only response was to open his little mouth and look at me expectantly.

The second telegram brought even better news: John would be having short leave at the end of the month. The visit to Finnart would be a brief one to discharge cargo, followed by a trip to Swansea to load fuel oil. They would discharge half of this at Finnart and half at Dingle Jetty on the River Mersey below Liverpool. From there they would head to Swansea for engine repairs. He was hoping this would give him chance to slip away to spend a day or two with Barbara and the baby. Barbara was delighted:

My excitement over yesterday's telegram was as nothing compared with the delight at today's telegram. Oh, dearest, I cannot tell you how much I am longing to be with you.

John was passing the time darning socks, removing marks from his battle-dress, sewing on buttons and ironing. He had thrown away socks and underpants that were past further mending, so he needed to do some shopping. He also needed a haircut:

At present I look like Robinson Crusoe and most of the other officers are likewise.

He telephoned Barbara from Finnart, where her letters awaited him. For the first time he learnt the details of Michael's birth:

Oh, my precious one, I wish I could have taken away some of your pain while Michael was being born. You are a very brave girl as well as being the dearest girl in the world to me.

'The Finger of Suspicion' (Finnart to Liverpool)

Meanwhile John had also been experiencing trying times. He told her on the phone about a collision on the way to Finnart:

It was about 3 am when I first saw this ship coming down fine on our starboard bow. It was her duty to keep out of the way, so I just kept on until she began to get dangerously close. I saw then that there would be a collision unless I did something about it, so after first whistling down for the captain, I went hard to Starboard and sounded one short blast. All this time the other ship could have easily cleared us by altering to Starboard, but instead she altered to Port just after we altered and so came heading towards us still. It was too late then for me to try going to Port, all I could do was to try to slow our ship down by ringing the engines full astern and keep swinging to Starboard. Soon after, the other ship hit our port bow, but by this time we were on only slightly convergent courses, so he struck a glancing blow and dropped rapidly astern. When clear we discovered the other ship was the 'Bjorn Clausen', a Danish ship bound to the Canary Islands. She reported only superstructure damage and our damage was confined to some bent rails and plates on the forecastle head.

We were soon on our way again, but we found the Radar wouldn't work, so I spent most of the morning on that. The worst of it was that snow had reduced visibility down to about a mile or less, so we couldn't proceed very fast without the Radar. We arrived at Finnart about 4pm and had soon made fast and were ready to pump the cargo ashore. No sooner had we made fast than the Superintendent came down and wanted to know all about the accident. I was also busy paying out money to the crew, overhauling the gyro and attending to the cargo, so I had a busy evening.

The snow also interfered with the phone line when John rang Barbara. She was hoping the enquiry into the collision would not prevent John coming home during his short leave at Falmouth. Ready if necessary to risk travelling with baby Michael, she was now back at her mother's house. Her brother's trawler had also been in a collision, with more serious consequences as two of the other crew had been killed. There was a possibility of their skipper being charged with manslaughter, and there was a risk that the crew might be out of a ship. However, the enquiry was postponed so they were soon back at sea on the same trawler. Despite the collision, the trip had been successful, and the markets were high, so Barbara's brother and his family now had a television. It cost £78.

Barbara's youngest brother, Donald, had been to the dentist with tooth-ache and had been told that all his teeth would have to come out and be replaced by false ones. He was twenty-one.

Barbara meanwhile was feeling the cold when sitting up in bed to give Michael his night feeds and was making sure there was always a hot water bottle in the cot. It was his own special bottle, a little pink one with a picture of 'Rock-a-bye Baby' on the side. John sent her a surprise present of a Pye Polly 'teas-made', which meant that she could boil water to refill the hot water bottle in the night without getting up. However, she needed to put a coat on every time she went to the outside toilet. On the plus side, Barbara was cheered up by being able to squeeze into a corset so that she could look slim again and was convinced that Michael was a child prodigy in the making:

When I was bathing him this morning, he dug his heels in and tried to stand up, and I have to hold him tightly when he is lying on my lap, as he sometimes nearly shoots himself off. I am half inclined to think he was post-mature, and that we had not miscalculated his birth date. But perhaps he is just a very special little boy and is going to be clever like his Daddy.

Although John was able to telephone again from Swansea and on his return to Finnart, Barbara was missing him more than ever, especially now that he was so near:

I am getting very impatient to see you again my dearest. It seems such an awfully long time since you sailed, and since you last kissed me. I can still see every detail of that Tuesday morning, in my mind. I felt as though my heart was breaking as I watched you sail away.

Suddenly, she couldn't bear it any longer. On the spur of the moment, she took three-and-a-half-week-old Michael on a train to Liverpool, so that they could spend a weekend with John while the British Guardian was berthed at Dingle Jetty. Both her mother and mother-in-law were waiting at the station when she returned, to check that mother and baby were back safe and sound. Then, before long, John did indeed get his short leave. He came home for several days, which included Michael's christening, and then they both returned to Falmouth to stay on the ship while it was in dock. Altogether they were able to spend two weeks together.

'Dreamboat' (Falmouth to Venezuela)

The taxi-driver was very tactful and kept up a stream of one-sided conversation to give me time to regain my composure after leaving you.

With the baby in a carrycot, Barbara travelled by train from Falmouth to Truro, where she was glad of the big coal fires in the waiting room, and then to London, before changing trains again for Hull. She had both lunch and afternoon tea brought to her in the compartment. Back in Hull she was met by deep snow and bitterly cold weather, but her first action was to send John a telegram assuring him of her safe arrival.

Despite three blankets and a hot water bottle, she was finding the nights very cold, especially without John to warm her up. She was grateful for the Pye Polly so that she could have a cup of tea before getting up in the morning, and she wrote her letters to John sitting on a cushion in front of the fire, looking at the vase of daffodils he had bought for her while he was home.

Barbara had left John a cake, various bars of chocolate, her toothbrush and face flannel, and a loving note. Michael had left him three nappies, which he washed and hung up in the cabin to dry. He was less thorough when it came to washing his own towel:

I noticed some of your lipstick on the towel so when I washed it I didn't rub that part very hard and now whenever I see it, it will remind me of the lovely weekend we had down in Falmouth.

His personal hygiene had however taken a turn for the better: '*I have had two baths in four days!*' While the ship headed towards Carapito, in Venezuela, he was reading a book on dreams and nightmares:

It seems to be quite a good book, but some of the claims it puts forward are I think a bit far-reaching. I certainly think that in dreams you can sometimes dream of what is happening at that time to the person you love, and I also think dreams can be a clue to our own inner tensions. On the other hand, I don't think dreams can foretell a happening unless the person dreaming knows that there is a likelihood of that particular event happening.

Meanwhile, Barbara was having some disquieting dreams back home:

I woke up once during the night feeling really jealous dearest, for I dreamed you had three very attractive passengers on the ship, and when I came to join you, you still continued to favour them with your attentions, and I was left all on my own. However, I knew as soon as I was properly awake that such a thing would only happen in a dream (I am not being presumptuous, am I dearest?) and soon went off to sleep again.

John replied:

You know me better than for me to shower my attention on women passengers. A common advert says, 'there is none better than the best' and I have the best wife in all the world.

Soon, Barbara decided that it was time to 'shorten' Michael, changing him out of nighties and into dresses during the daytime, so that he would know that he could play during the day but must sleep at night:

What a sweet little pet he looked, although I think he took rather a dim view of it all, judging by the look he gave me when I was dressing him. To give you an idea of what he was wearing on this important day: a vest, bodice, nappy, winceyette petticoat, silk petticoat, the dress you bought, bootees, and a little wool coat. I wish you could have seen him, dearest.

Now she was starting to think about potty-training him, although she was probably being rather optimistic:

While I was rubbing Michael's back to bring his wind up after the 6pm feed, he tried to put the fire out, and his aim was very good! Soon he will have done it everywhere but in his potty.

Michael had started on cod liver oil and rosehip syrup. Mother and son were both declared fit and well at their six-week check-up. The doctor asked Barbara if the experience had put her off having any more children, but she said they were looking forward to having a second child. What she didn't know was what steps could be taken to avoid having another baby too soon:

Somehow it is not a subject which I discuss with friends. I wonder if men talk about it more freely – have you picked up any advice darling?

'Stranger in Paradise' (Venezuela to Swansea)

To his disappointment, John did not receive any of Barbara's many letters when he reached Carapito, three weeks after sailing from Falmouth. He described the town in his next letter:

Brightly coloured butterflies and birds flew round about us and little lizards scurried from our path, but in the rain we looked out for monkeys and alligators, which are supposed to abound around Carapito. Several of the crew swore they had seen alligators and at night you could hear the monkeys, but apart from a few monkeys in cages at the Seamen's club, that was the only indication of wild animal and reptile life. On the other hand, we saw numerous species of tropical birds – bright red, blue, yellow and green ones. Some like the preying condors were quite a size and others were much less in size than any English bird. Some of the birds built peculiar nests hanging down some 10 to 15 feet from the highest trees and in these swinging masses of grass and reeds the birds made their home. Two bright green and yellow birds had made their nests in the head of the crane on the wharf we were alongside and on another part of the crane some hornets had made a nest and all day long these big insects came whizzing by taking food to help build up the honeycomb.

He was delighted to get the message 'Land's End for Orders' and sent a telegram to Barbara to say that they were heading back from Carapito to Swansea. Although it might only be a brief visit, at least he would be able to telephone from there. As they sailed, he was busy with his washing and mending:

The pile of dirty washing is gradually increasing so tomorrow I expect I shall have to make a start on that. At Carapito I dirtied up a pair of white shorts and shirt with fuel oil, so I am wondering whether I shall be able to remove the stains. I dumped that very old pair of sandshoes but have cleaned up the other pair. The rubber soles needed repairing on a pair of my shoes and the soles were tending to part company with the uppers. They were soon repaired (after a fashion) so now they should last for a few more months, although the cobbling would certainly earn no medals.

He was also still thinking about the collision near Finnart:

When I take my next leave, I want to borrow the book 'Collisions at Sea' either from the Nautical School or through the library. After a collision, one's self-confidence receives rather a jolt, so I should like to look up a few cases of collisions just to see what actions the court approves in a case like that. Of course, on the other hand it isn't always the action the court approves that avoids a collision, but my mind would be easier if I read up about it.

Barbara was determined to travel down to Swansea to see John. She had not yet received any of his letters on this trip, so she made her own mind up:

If I don't hear anything, we shall just come – and hope you do not mind. I wonder if you will know we are coming. I have looked through our code, but we have not got a group for telling you that we are coming to you, even though there are groups telling me to come or not to come.

They had three happy days together before John set sail again. On the final night they went for a walk along the docks.

'Prize of Gold' – or silver (Swansea to Syria)

On March 16th, Barbara was again travelling back to Hull on the train after saying goodbye to her husband:

When I was at school, and used to go to Sheffield, I used to travel 'care of the guard'. Little did I think that some 10 to 15 years later I should be doing so again. When the porter took me along to the train, he put me in an empty Ladies Only compartment next to the luggage van and told the guard to 'keep an eye on this young lady and her baby, they are going to Hull via Gloucester.' When we arrived at Gloucester I found I had been very much in the guard's care, as he had locked me in to make sure no one else got in.

She got home to find that John had been awarded a Silver Medal by the Royal Society of Arts for his success in the Extra-Masters exam. She immediately sent him a telegram and then wrote:

I am so very pleased and proud dearest, but you deserve it for the way in which you studied, and now everyone will know what a clever husband I have got.

John replied:

I am afraid that while I was studying my studies took the larger share of my time and I was not able to give you all the attention you deserved. However, the results seem to have justified the sacrifices we made. I certainly don't think I could have achieved the success without a very happy home life – and you certainly made my life at home very happy. Also, you looked after me, cheered me up when I felt discouraged and helped me to really enjoy the times I was not studying. I think it was you who deserves the Silver Medal, dearest, not me.

Word soon got out. A couple of days later, Barbara had a visit from a Yorkshire Post reporter:

One question he asked stumped me, and that was where your ship is based. I said I did not know it was based anywhere, but he said every ship has its home base. He wanted to know where you had gone to and when you would be back, whether you knew about the award and what you thought about it. He also asked for a recent photograph of you in uniform, in case they have room to print it. The best ones of you are the wedding photographs, but they are all stuck in the album, so in the end I gave him the one taken before we were married, only it is not too special, as you are looking down. The report should be in tomorrow's paper, so I shall have to be out bright and early to get a couple of copies.

The next day, she continued:

You certainly are in the news today darling, for not only was there a report in the Yorkshire Post, but there is also one in the Hull Daily Mail. It was only by chance that I saw the one in the Mail as my visitor had left hers, and I was just casually looking through it when the headline 'Wins Silver Medal' caught my eye.

Barbara had been shopping to celebrate:

I had quite an expensive afternoon, and most of the money went on me, as I bought a mackintosh and some shoes. I bought the mac at Thornton's and it was only by chance I got it, as Mother had been in the shop and remarked that they were having a 'Special Offer' of raincoats. The one I got was 29/11d. It is red with a pattern in white on it and has a hat to match. It can be worn either belted or as a 'loose' coat, so it will be useful if Peter or Patricia is on the way.

My shoes were rather expensive, 69/9d, but they are a perfect fit, so the costs should be justified. They are brown calf leather, court style, with a medium heel.

Fortunately, John had just received a pay rise, his monthly pay increasing to £64-15-0, but he still had to make do and mend:

The day before yesterday I did a bit of sewing. You know those interlock underpants which I have that I was saying had stretched out of shape? Well

I decided to take a pleat up in either side so now they all fit reasonably well once again.

He didn't want Barbara to waste good money on his birthday present:

I am not fussy about what you get me, but if you do get a fountain pen, don't pay a lot for it. for I think it is scandalous the prices they charge for pens such as 'Parker 51' when actually a 1/6d ballpoint pen will probably do the job almost as good. Anyhow please yourself on what object you buy, but really you needn't buy me anything, for the best present I could have would be to return home to see you.

Meanwhile Barbara was watching the small back garden come back to life after the winter:

The fruit bushes and the lilac tree are in bud and the weeds are thriving. The grass seems in quite good condition but rather shaggy. I was wondering whether you would like a lawn mower for your birthday, darling?

It was now two years since they had met and they both sent each other telegrams to mark the occasion. On March 30th, John also wrote:

In a way I cannot believe that just over two years ago I hadn't met you, for now you are an essential part of me. Two years ago, I couldn't realise the amount of happiness that knowing you would bring to me and I hope I have made you happy too during this time. On the other hand, our time together has been all too brief...

John tried to occupy his mind by reading, his choice of books being as varied as ever: a collection of war-time Science broadcasts, a book on the value of scepticism by Bertrand Russell, and an article on 'Baby's First Year' in the Pears Cyclopaedia. Occasionally he took a break:

The other night I decided to have a lazy evening, so I went down to the smoke-room, settled in an easy chair and listened to the radio. At such times when I am not busy about the ship, my mind invariably wanders to thoughts about you and Baby, and I wondered whether you too would be listening to the radio. It made me think just how few really lazy evenings we have had together, for whilst I was home most of my evenings were spent studying and then of course when I wasn't studying there was visiting.

Barbara still spent a lot of time visiting. There were bus-trips to Beverley to see John's parents and sometimes she would spend the weekend with them, trying her best to keep up with her letter-writing:

Just in case I don't write sense, I should tell you that your dad is giving his views on what is to happen at the Second Coming, and every time I start to write he starts up again. I hope you get home before it happens because Dad says that Christians will just be translated! I have seen charts and maps and goodness knows what to prove what is to happen. Both Mother and I are trying to write to you, but Dad is very persistent! By the way, Mother does not believe in birth control, so I trust you know what she thinks we should – or rather should not – do for the next two years!

John responded:

I can see Dad is making the most of lack of opposition to lecture on the Second Coming. However, it is just one of those things it is hard to discuss either logically or sensibly as some people have very strong convictions regarding it and of course are biased. I am looking forward to discussing religion when I come home next for we shall have to decide what we are going to teach or allow to be taught to Michael.

He made no comment on his mother's advice on birth control. John's father took Barbara to see the film 'Lease of Life' at the Playhouse in Beverley:

So darling, I have been out with another man, but as it was your father I do not think you need to be jealous. I enjoyed the film very much, because, apart from the local setting, the story was unusual. Dad enjoyed it but was disappointed at seeing so few local people in it.

He would not have been disappointed however by the reception he and Barbara received as they walked through the town:

It seems we are the talk of the town, for about half of Beverley stopped Dad to say they have seen the newspaper reports and photographs. It was a good job it happened last week and not this, as the newspaper trade is on strike and there have been no newspapers since Friday. Strikes seem to be in the air at the moment as the dockers are also on strike.

John's mother showed her pictures of John as a baby and small child:

On two of the older ones, you look like a sweet little girl darling! I was quite surprised to know they were of my handsome husband.

Barbara obviously met with the approval of her in-laws. John wrote:

Even my mother remarked in one of her letters what a good mother you are – and praise from the mother-in-law is praise indeed.

Barbara also regularly walked to Hessle with the pram to see her mother and to visit her sister-in-law. The new television was a big attraction and she watched Andy Pandy with Michael and her nieces:

I think it is one of the best TV programmes, even if it is strictly for the under-fives.

There were birthday parties for her nieces:

We had quite good fun playing 'Oranges and Lemons', 'Ring-a-ring-o-roses' and 'Poor Mary sat a weeping'.

She was keen to show Michael off in public:

Michael attended his first social event today, and he was a great success. We went to an American Tea at the Mission to Seamen, where they showed a very interesting film about some of the work of the Mission. Michael sat on my knee all the time and fell asleep just before the raffle was drawn, so I put him in his carry-cot. I think almost all the ladies came to admire our son, but his greatest admirers were Sir Arthur Atkinson and Captain Grimston. Sir Arthur gave him a kiss and said he was a fine boy, and Captain Grimston asked if he was going to be a Captain and win great honours like his Daddy. Several of the ladies also sent their congratulations to you on winning the Silver Medal. I am really bursting with pride in my clever husband, but not only are you very clever dearest you are the best, kindest and most loving husband in all the world.

I made some butterfly buns for the American Tea and although I wondered how they would turn out they were really quite nice, and I noticed they went very quickly. Of course, we may hear that a dozen or so ladies have been violently sick tonight!

'Every Day of My Life'

Reading remained John's chief leisure pastime:

> The library has just opened so I have been down to change my last two books.
> They were 'The Hell Bomb' and 'Russia and the Russians', the former being
> about the hydrogen bomb and the second being sociological. Now I have a
> book out in a lighter vein, 'None but the Lonely Heart' (a different type of
> book from what I normally read). My heart too is lonely – lonely for you
> Darling.
>
> By the way, how is the fire-grate coming on?

Always, amidst the romance, there are thoughts of a more practical nature:

> You can touch up the paintwork if you like but quite a lot of painting will
> need to be done when I come home on leave. Before I paint the dining room
> I think it will be best to go over the previous paintwork with a pumice-stone
> and that will soon even out any irregularities.

Barbara however decided it was best to leave it well alone:

> I don't think I will do anything at all to the paintwork except wash it, for I am
> not very good with the paintbrush, and it is only a waste of good paint. So, I
> will leave all the painting for you to do, darling.

She continued to keep track of her expenditure:

> I wrote up my housekeeping book. It has been an expensive week this week,
> as I have spent £7.3.8½d since April 1st. £2.15.0 was on food, the balance
> being miscellaneous expenditure. The main items were Easter presents, shoe
> repairs, and postage. On the food side, my biggest expenditure is on fruit and
> vegetables. I think the rest of the month will be fairly moderate. In March I
> kept more or less to the £17 which we allowed for housekeeping.

Housework filled much of her time and was a cure for the 'blues' that she was
feeling after not hearing from John for so long.:

> I really must make a start on spring cleaning, but until the last few days, the
> weather has not been very encouraging. Next week, being Easter week, will be
> a short week, so I don't think I shall start any cleaning in a big way, although
> I may start on drawers etc. Today after I had finished the washing I did all
> the outside paintwork, back and front (downstairs only, of course). Then I

'dusted' the staircase with a damp cloth, and washed the window ledges and skirtings in here, and dusted the rest of the room. Next, I swept and washed the bathroom, kitchenette and veranda floors, and so once again everything is clean.

John was also trying to keep up with his chores:

Yesterday I did quite a large wash but when it came to ironing them, I fused the circuit a couple of times. I took the iron apart to see what could have caused the fuse and I came to the conclusion that one of the wires must have been touching the body of the iron. Anyway, after I had put the iron back together again it went all right and this morning I was able to do all my ironing.

After Easter, Barbara started on the spring cleaning:

I decided that as it was a very nice day I would start with the two back bedrooms, so I set to work on them. It took me until 3.30pm but by then I had the clean curtains hung up again, and both bedrooms smelling sweetly and looking very nice.

The next day, she continued:

I took the stair carpet up except for the corner, and I thought if I undid that I might not get it back again, so I shall have to do that when you come home sometime. When I was putting the carpet down again, I was an underfelt short, so I had to use one of the spare ones… I had quite a job getting some of the stair rods back in.

After spring-cleaning the lounge until after 9 o'clock at night, Barbara wrote:

The room certainly looks better for being cleaned, but I feel a bit tired now. I am sure I could not do such heavy work over a period, as our mothers seem to do, and yet I am far from weak – I don't think I am lazy, but there must be some explanation.

She was also trying to keep Michael looking presentable:

He will probably keep a bit tidier in rompers, as he has reached the stage now when he is constantly putting his dress into his mouth, and his clean dress only looks clean for about ten minutes, so he is being changed twice a day if we are going out.

She continued to be very proud of his development:

> *I had Michael weighed today and he was exactly 15lbs 8oz in his dress and matinee coat, so he has gained about two pounds in the last month. I have filled in his weight on the graph sent by the Motherhood Circle, and his weight line runs almost parallel to the specimen average line, so he is evidently gaining the right amount. The same leaflet says that at three months a baby should begin to 'grasp at objects, coos, gurgles, babbles, kicks in pen.' Michael does that, although he doesn't have a pen to kick in, but he kicks well on the settee, and can move backwards quite quickly.*

He too had appeared in the newspaper:

> *It would seem that our family cannot keep out of the news, for the enclosed photograph was on the front page of the Mail tonight. Mrs Cleveland called over to see if we had seen it, and said we are making Westfield Road quite famous. I think it is a lovely picture of Michael, don't you darling?*

John's response, when he received the cutting, was:

> *I like the photo of Michael and you, but it looks as if Michael is taking a dim view of all the goings on. We have certainly succeeded in getting our names and pictures in the papers a few times during the last two years.*

'I wonder' (Syria to Philadelphia)

The British Guardian had loaded cargo at Banias in Syria and was crossing the North Atlantic on its way to Philadelphia:

> *This morning a flight of American bombers passed high overhead bound for Europe and I expect that as I write this letter they will have already arrived at their bases in England or on the continent. I wish I could get home just as quick.*

Barbara had not yet received any letters from John and was hoping that when he did return it would not be to a continental port until she got her passport back with Michael added to it:

> *I had a letter from the passport office requesting me to 'forward a letter from the father, as legal guardian, consenting to the grant of passport facilities to the child'. As you see, they will not put Michael's particulars on my passport until they receive a letter from you – to make sure I do not run away with him.*

She had been looking up Philadelphia on the map:

> *I really am beginning to learn some Geography at last! You have no idea just how ignorant I was about the position of different countries to each other. I sometimes am surprised myself at my ignorance and wonder how I managed to learn so little at school. No wonder I did not pass Geography on the School Certificate exam. Now I have looked at the map I see Philadelphia is nearer the UK than Banias, so it should not take you so long to get back, but I shall try not to count on it.*

The letter that John sent from Banias had gone astray and Barbara was feeling increasingly forlorn. It never did arrive. She sent him a telegram on Easter Day to send her love and to let him know that she had not heard from him yet. John replied in a letter:

> *Perhaps it has been sent by sea-mail by mistake. In case you don't receive it however there was nothing in it of outstanding importance except to tell you that I love you more than anyone else in the world and to thank you for giving me such a lovely three days in Swansea.*

He was hoping that he had decoded her telegram correctly:

> *I took ZLZO to mean 'have not received letters', although of course ZOH could mean 'not all well'.*

When he reached Philadelphia on April 15th, there were seven letters waiting for him. He decided not to go ashore as it would cost around 30/- for the return taxi fare:

> *Today I asked two people to bring me stamps back from Philadelphia and one returned sober, so I hope to be able to post this letter tomorrow.*

After five weeks of separation, Barbara had received two telegrams but no letters. One day her hopes were raised when the postman called but were soon dashed when she realised he had only delivered a Persil coupon. She could hear some neighbours having an argument:

> *They have just been having a terrific row and the language has been rather bad. I don't know what had gone wrong, but they certainly were not very polite to each other.*

The same neighbour later cornered Barbara:

She told me quite a lot of their personal affairs, which I would have preferred her not to, but she seemed to want to get it off her chest. She said she wished her boys had married 'a nice girl like you'.

April 20th was D-Day, when John's long-awaited letter finally arrived. She read it four or five times and it made her very happy:

Thank you dearest for all the nice things you said in your letter. I hope I shall always be able to justify them, and to make you happy. That is what I want to do more than anything else, and next to that I want to be a good mother to our dear little Michael. He certainly has got the best father that any child could have, and if he takes after you, he should grow into a very nice, intelligent, kind and thoughtful boy, as well as being a very handsome one.

'If You Believe' (Philadelphia to the Cape Verde Islands)

From Philadelphia, the British Guardian headed for Curacao in the Dutch West Indies. John was looking through his photo album:

The other day I went through my photo album fixing on corner holders. However, I was about 30 short, so if you could slip some in one of your letters I could certainly utilise them.

He had been glancing through a newsletter from the Anglo-Iranian Oil Company (now BP):

There was quite a paragraph about my silver medal and a short account of my time in the company. I was glad it didn't mention the collision, though. I haven't heard any more about the collision but when I am home on leave, if we go down to London, I shall call in at Britannic House and see how the case is progressing.

Although I have had various congratulations about the RSA award, the queerest one was last night when the British Mariner signalled us during the Third Mate's watch and asked him to pass on their congratulations.

Recent increases in wages in the Merchant Navy meant that John's wages might increase soon to around £68 per month, but he was still considering future career options:

Even if we have to make a few sacrifices so that I can be home I feel it will be worth it to be with you most of the time. I don't particularly agree with Dad that teaching is a particularly inferior job, but I do think there are better jobs, only most of them need additional qualifications.

For the time being however he would probably stay at sea, although he was looking at the possibility of trips that would return home more frequently. Barbara could see that this might be sensible, but replied:

I do feel though darling that if you are staying at sea, it would be better to confine our children to two only, as to have more would rather hamper my chances of joining you at any time. After all, although I am sure both of our parents would be very pleased to look after one or two children for a short while, it is a bit much to ask them to look after half a dozen!

At the port of Willemstad in Curacao, the British Guardian loaded cargo for Porto Grande on the Island of St Vincent in the Cape Verde islands, off the West Coast of Africa. When they arrived, John stayed on board ship:

Apparently, all there was to offer ashore was wine, women and song, with the emphasis on the first two, so I stayed and helped the drunks back on board. I am certainly glad I am still not a 'bachelor gay' for I am far more happy and contented than I was before we were married.

He was pleased to receive three more letters from Barbara, but disappointed to hear that the letters he had sent from Banias had never reached her. He was concerned to hear that Barbara had been losing her hair and teeth whilst breastfeeding:

It will certainly be wise for you to go and see the doctor about some calcium tablets. Do look after yourself dearest for you are everything to me. I shall still love you no matter how bald or gummy you are, but I should rather you went to see the doctor and dentist to arrest it now. Remember that although I love Baby Michael a lot, my love for you is incomparably greater. So do take care of yourself my darling and don't stint yourself for any type of food which would help to replace the minerals that you are giving Baby just because it would run the housekeeping over the mark we set.

The doctor prescribed iron and thyroid tablets, together with a large bottle of liquid paraffin. Barbara did not say what it was to be used for. Meanwhile, the General Election had been called for May 26th and Barbara had obtained a proxy vote for John:

We are now in the West Hull constituency, but I think there will only be Labour and Conservative candidates. So far as I know, the Liberals are only fighting Haltemprice in this area, so what do you want me to vote for you?

John asked Barbara to obtain the party manifestos for him. He was aware that there had been a number of party political broadcasts on the radio, but he hadn't heard any of them:

Before I went to sea I was intensely interested in the news, but I suppose that at sea it seems to affect us so very little and also even with a radio it is not always easy to get the BBC news when you want it. Of course, you can usually get news broadcasts from America or Russia, but they are that full of propaganda and that sifted that one feels inclined to switch them off straight away.

This was a time of increasing polarisation during the Cold War between the USA and the Soviet Union. West Germany had just joined NATO and started to rearm, while the Soviet Union and Eastern Bloc countries were founding the Warsaw Pact as a Communist counterpart to NATO. Barbara was only able to obtain the Tory manifesto, so she sent that to John. The recent tax-cutting budget had proved popular with the public:

According to the Gallup Polls, the Conservatives have 2½ % majority so I think they will get in again. This is the quietest General Election I have known. I have not seen one poster or any literature at all. It seems the various parties are depending on the radio and television to put over their propaganda, so very few meetings are being held.

John decided in the end that Barbara should vote Conservative for him, although he felt it would not make much difference as he thought the constituency was a safe Conservative seat. Maybe he was thinking they were still part of the Haltemprice constituency. In fact, there had been a number of changes for the 1955 General Election. The Liberal-voting Hull West and Hessle constituency had been abolished in 1918 and then recreated in 1955. It returned a Labour MP and would remain firmly Labour-voting until it was abolished under further boundary changes in 1997.

Meanwhile John was going through a period of doubting his religious faith:

At the present I am feeling rather disillusioned as I have been going through the various beliefs of the Church of England and asking myself why I believed in each Article. In the end I find that there are very few Articles of Religion as set down in the Prayer Book that I do believe in. On the other hand, it is easy to find faults with the Church's beliefs but incomparably harder to substitute better beliefs. It is that easy to separate one's life into separate watertight compartment: one for religion, one for ordinary life and one for scientific thought. For instance, suppose someone burgled our house we should ordinarily want our goods back, but the New Testament on which our religious beliefs are based says that if someone steals your hat you should give them your coat also. Several Christian beliefs are based on the story of Adam and Eve and yet if we study Archaeology we accept quite different views of the Creation. It all leaves me very much confused much in the same way as does a study of Political Economics. However perhaps we shall sort some of these things out when I am home on leave next.

Barbara replied:

Your remarks gave me something to think about while I was washing and cleaning out the pantry, and I found that the only reason I believe in quite a lot of things is because I had always been taught it from being quite small, and so accepted the facts without any question. I soon was deep in thought, and found myself wondering about God, about evolution, and how everything started in the beginning. How did God get there to begin with? I certainly should try to sort out some of the questions.

Did I tell you I say the prayer 'Gentle Jesus' to Michael every night now? I am sure he knows and waits for it after I have tucked him in and kissed him 'Goodnight from Daddy' and 'Goodnight from Mummy'.

'The Breeze and I' (St Vincent to Iran)

After discharging their cargo at St Vincent, the British Guardian sailed within sixty miles of the Canary Islands, as they headed towards the Mediterranean. Even from that distance it was possible to make out the silhouettes of the mountains. They skirted the coast of North Africa, heading towards Port Said and still awaiting further orders. In the hope that they might soon return to the UK, John was giving his cases a coat of black paint prior to painting his name and address on them, as they still had his parents address in Beverley.

The orders eventually came to load a cargo of fuel oil at Abadan in Iran, taking it to Mina-al-Ahmadi in Kuwait, some fifty miles away. There they would be loading crude oil and heading to 'Land's End for Orders', although there was no guarantee of returning to a UK port. Barbara was delighted to receive the news in a telegram. She intercepted the telegraph boy riding his motorbike towards their house, just as she was about to catch a bus:

> I dashed inside for the code and as I had no time to decode the telegram before the bus came, I did it as soon as I sat down. I am sure the passengers must have noticed how happy I became when I found that XX stood for Land's End for Orders. Of course, I told Michael that Daddy was coming home soon, and he chuckled just as though he understood. I feel quite a different person – all my former depression has gone now I have a date – even though it is only an approximate one – when I can hope to see you again.

There were nine further letters waiting for John at Port Said on the Suez Canal. Barbara had expressed surprise at how helpful she found the porters to be whenever she travelled by train:

> I can't make up my mind about the reason. Is it because I look helpless, or is it because they like the way I look? Whatever it is, I certainly get results.

John replied:

> I think the porters must like the way you look. In any case I like the way you look far better than anyone else in the world. On the other hand, perhaps, the porters can tell that you appreciate their help whereas other people often don't seem to.

With temperatures of 90% in the shade, John needed to cool down with a 'dip and splash' in the Suez Canal:

> It was quite refreshing but very salty.

He was finding it hard to sleep at night when he was often drenched in sweat, finally falling asleep just a few hours before it was time to be up again. He was quite looking forward to visiting Abadan, as he had never been there:

> Still I don't expect that I shall go ashore unless it is to the swimming pool or the canteen for I don't want to test the friendliness of the Persians.

It was only two years since the government of Iran had been overthrown by an Anglo-American covert operation. This coup d'état deposed the Prime Minister who had achieved popularity by nationalising Iran's petroleum industry and oil reserves. The nights continued to be hot:

Last night when I turned in there was a strong breeze blowing through my ports, so I had to close them. After I had gone to sleep the breeze abated and I woke up at 10.30 to find the room unbearably hot. I then opened the ports again and turned in until it was time to go on watch at midnight, by which time the breeze had started up again and my room was a shambles of papers blowing about all over.

Arriving at Abadan, John decided to go ashore after all:

The Old Man was going out to tea, so we had a lift up to the town in his car. As we had no Persian money I changed two English pounds and got quite a good rate of exchange. I also managed to buy a film for my camera so perhaps I shall be taking some snaps soon. When we arrived at the club the Mate started drinking double whiskys, and although I ordered beer one time and a soft drink another, the waiter seemed to think we should be drinking whisky and each time faithfully brought along two whiskys. This made the drinks rather dear, so I ended up spending more than I had intended. At half past eight however a film was being shown at the open-air cinema of the club, so we went in to see it. The film was called 'Painting the clouds with sunshine' and was a light-hearted musical comedy. It helped to pass the evening quite pleasantly and I was glad of a break in the drinking. The club wasn't far from the ship and as the journey back was through the refinery all the way, we walked back. Apparently, it is considered quite safe to walk through the native quarter, but we didn't fancy it at night.

Whilst I was ashore I kept thinking how nice it would have been if you had been with me. There were quite a lot of Iranian families at the club and their children were playing on a roundabout and on the grass. I was wondering whether in a couple of years we shall be taking Michael for rides on children's roundabouts and whether he will be asking for pennies for ice-cream, like some of the children at the club were asking their parents. I always seem to miss you most when I am ashore, for when I see a film my mind wanders back to the last time we were at the cinema together; when I go shopping I think of the last time we went shopping together; and I am constantly being reminded of little things we have done together. Perhaps the various things I see and do on board are more associated in my mind with work, but pleasure is certainly associated in my mind with you my dearest for I am never happier than when I am with you.

Barbara was concerned that John's parents were struggling financially. John's father, now aged 70, had a pension of £3-5-0, which he supplemented by teaching occasional shorthand lessons in his own home. Her mother-in-law had told Barbara that she wouldn't be visiting her other son in Ross-on-Wye this year:

> *I have an idea that it is for financial reasons that she is doubtful of going, because I know she wants to see them very much, and it does not look as though they will get over to Beverley. I wondered if we could help them with regard to the fare, darling? If you think it is a good idea perhaps you could mention it in one of your letters to them, but don't let them think I have said anything about it, or Mother might not talk to me as freely as she does at present. I think at the moment their financial position is rather under a strain, as Mother needs some shoes and Dad needs some flannels. I have grown very fond of them both, and I should like us to help them a bit if it is possible – I hope you do not think I am interfering, darling.*

She was thinking they would soon need to be buying a big cot for Michael:

> *I would rather he was 'behind bars' as soon as he can sit up on his own. Your mother said she used to spread cushions around the floor in case you fell out, but I think it would be less of a strain to make certain he was safe, don't you?*

With the weather warming up, Barbara had bought a sun-canopy for Michael's pram and was pleased with the effect:

> *I wore my grey costume, white blouse and new hat, and Mother said I looked very nice. I certainly felt very proud of Michael and his pram. Michael was all in white, and his white eiderdown and pillow made a contrast to his navy pram and canopy. The outside of the pram literally shone, as I had given it an extra good clean this morning. I went tripping along Anlaby Road, showing off my pram, when a small gust of wind blew something into my eye, and for the rest of the way I could only keep one eye open – perhaps that is what comes of being vain!*

It must have been a relief to dress up smartly and go out, after a day at home doing the housework:

> *I do not remember whether I have mentioned in previous letters about the large number of various types of insects which abound in the veranda. In an endeavour to find where they were coming from, I picked up the corner of the*

floor canvas, and sure enough, there was the breeding ground. The canvas was very mouldy too, so I took it all up. It seems that fresh lino must have been put down each time one lot went fusty, because in some places there were three lots, and all of it mouldy and rotten. The concrete was absolutely filthy, with hundreds of insects, nests etc, so I stood at the door and threw several buckets of water on the floor, and then gave it a very good scrub with the yard brush. I repeated this treatment several times, until I was fairly certain that all the insects had been drowned or brushed away. After dinner I continued along the rest of the veranda, then finished off by giving the floor another swill with disinfectant water, so it should be better now. The concrete is in very bad condition, but I think it is better to leave it uncovered rather than put fresh lino down. I do think the floor needs some covering, though, and those old strips are carpeting are not much good, so I will have a look round to see what I can find in the shops. I think we just need two strips of carpet, one between the wringer, cooker and copper, and the sink, and another from the main door to the wall.

'Learnin' the Blues' (Iran to Kuwait)

John was heading back along the Shatt-al Arab river towards their discharging port of Mena-al-Ahmadi:

The river waters are led off on both sides of the river for irrigation. Hence the land on either side of the river for two or three miles in width is honeycombed with these small irrigation channels. This strip of land is therefore quite fertile and plantations of date palms line both banks most of the way up the river.

Little did John know that this date palm forest, the largest in the world, would have millions of its trees destroyed in the next fifty years by war, salt and pests. The conflicting claims to navigational rights along this river was one of the causes of the Iran-Iraq war in the 1980s. Back in 1954, however, all was peaceful:

The river is kept from flooding the land by low dykes but in places the land is not enclosed and is used by the Iranians for growing paddy (rice), the ground for this crop needing to be waterlogged for a good proportion of the time. We passed several villages and noticed most of the houses seem to be built of clay, some with clay-covered roofs and some just covered with palm leaves. When we went up the river it was a Mohammedan holiday, so all the women and children were out wearing their best clothes. Normally the women wear black robes from head to foot, but I noticed for the holiday some of them wore bright clothes underneath and the children were running about in bright reds and greens.

Meanwhile Barbara was sitting up to hear the first election results come in:

At the last election Mother and I slept downstairs on the bed settee and listened in throughout the night. According to the reports the poll has been about 88%, and a high poll usually favours Labour, so I am now wondering what the outcome will be. I wonder if you will be listening in to the results, as various countries are broadcasting them. Cheltenham just coming through – Conservative, with an increased majority of nearly 2000. The Liberals (including one of my Young Liberal friends) have lost three deposits so far, and not got a seat yet. Sir Anthony Eden has increased his majority by 4000.

John had indeed listened to the results:

As I write this letter there is a cricket chirruping away in my cabin, so I hope it goes before I turn in. Although I can hear it, I don't seem to be able to find it. Earlier today I listened to the election results – it seems the Conservatives are in once more.

Barbara gave more detail about local results the next day:

In our constituency, West Hull, the labour candidate got in with a majority of only 5000. The Haltemprice Conservative doubled his majority.

In fact, the Conservatives remained in power throughout the nineteen-fifties, from Sir Winston Churchill's defeat of Clement Atlee in 1951, up to Harold Wilson taking over from Sir Alec Douglas Home as Prime Minister in 1964. Despite the legacy of the war years, rationing was finally coming to an end, and the nineteen-fifties were seen as a time of economic growth, leading Harold Macmillan to make his famous statement in 1957 that 'most of our people have never had it so good'.

Things didn't seem quite so good in the aftermath of the 1955 election. On June 1st, Barbara wrote:

With the conditions in England as they are at present, I cannot see BTC sending any ships to UK ports, for half the dockers are on strike, a large proportion of the railway workers are also on strike, and today a state of emergency has been proclaimed. Everyone is wondering how long the strike will last, and some say it will be like the general strike in 1926. Already the electricity supply has been affected, and the power is much less than usual. There is also only one postal delivery a day.

There were six letters waiting for John at Mena-al-Ahmadi. He was impressed to hear of the progress Michael was making:

Certainly, all his progressive actions should be encouraged, for I think even boys of his age derive satisfaction through having achieved something. Babies don't usually get tired or whimpery through doing things they want to do but they do through fretting if they are frustrated too often.

'Ready, Willing and Able' (Kuwait to Swansea)

From Mena, the ship headed back towards Suez through the Red Sea. The weather was particularly warm and humid:

I have been having a rip-roaring time with some of my shirts again. I think sweating must cause them to rot, for the most trivial exertion seems to tear them, and another two of my shirts have been consigned to the deep.

His reading matter however had been about cooler climes:

I have now finished that book on the 'Frozen North' and I was surprised at the primitive way in which the natives live in Northern Canada, even in quite recent times (1940). Cleanliness and higher ideals seem to have been put aside in the fight for survival.

John himself was not famed for his love of personal cleanliness however. He replied to Barbara's description of Michael's bath-time:

He seems to have a grand time in the bath and perhaps he will take after his Mummy as far as washing goes. I know one of his grandparents who will be pleased if he does.

John had some sewing to do:

I started to stitch BTC braid and buttons on my old uniform. As it looks as if I shall be in the company a while yet, I thought that perhaps after all I should have their braid up, especially as it is provided free. I am afraid I was in rather a hurry, so the stitching is terrible but perhaps it may look all right at the distance a superintendent might see it.

While he was sewing his uniform, Barbara was doing the smocking on a pair of rompers she was making for Michael ready for the summer. Occasionally however she would buy him an outfit:

> I bought Michael a sweet little 'carrying' coat today. It is in white crepe silk, lined with taffeta, and has six buttons on the yoke, to give a double-breasted look, smocking just below the yoke, and has lace trimming on the collar. It cost £1-1-0 and I know I could have made one like it, but I should only have saved about three shillings, and I could not see me getting it done it time.

They had been out in the June sunshine:

> How I envy you and Michael, for whereas you both go brown, I just burn, and tonight my face, neck and wrists are bright red.

But the sun was short-lived:

> Tonight, I am wearing a cardigan, and sitting almost on top of the fire to keep warm.

She was wondering whether to stop Michael's night feed:

> I decided that as he had had a feed just after 10 pm I would only give him water if he woke up during the early hours. Michael did wake about 3.45 am. so I gave him several spoonfuls of boiled water, changed him and put him back in his cot. He made no murmur but gave me such a reproachful and hurt look it nearly broke my heart and I was tempted to pick him up again. However, I hardened my heart and waited to see if he would settle. You have no idea how I felt darling. I worried whether he was really hungry and whether he was feeling unhappy. Every few minutes he would give a little cry and then stop and suck his thumb very noisily. After a quarter of an hour I gave in and picked him up and gave him a small feed. So now I am wondering what to do. I think I really should persevere and break him off that feed, but it hurts me to do it. I wish you were here darling to reassure me that I am doing the right thing.

By now she was desperate to know which port John was heading for and had found out the fares to all the continental ports, just in case. A return fare ranged from £8 for Rotterdam to £20 for Copenhagen:

> I would gladly starve for the next few weeks to repay the travelling expenses out of the housekeeping money!

Despite Barbara's anxiety over the night feed, Michael seems to have been happy in his own little world:

His favourite playthings at the moment are his toes., and he will sit almost doubled up clutching his toes, and when I am feeding him I have to cover them up, otherwise he stops feeding to play with them. He is the sauciest baby I ever saw and laughs and chuckles at any time of the day or night. He also squeals and blows bubbles, if he has an audience who is willing to praise him. Who said men were not the vainest sex?

On 16th June, Barbara received the long-awaited telegram to inform her that the British Guardian would be calling at a UK port. Barbara travelled with the Second Engineer's wife on the overnight boat train from London to Dunkirk and then sailed with John round to Swansea, where they spent a week together, before the ship sailed again towards Port Said with a new captain.

'Cool Water' (Swansea to Kuwait)

It was clear from the start that John and the captain would not see eye-to-eye:

The new Captain seems to have quite a number of ideas of his own and likes everything done his way. He also takes a very active part in the navigation of the ship. This is all very well providing it doesn't interfere too much with my methods. Sometimes however I draw the line. He told us he had a much more accurate method of working up the day's distance and hinted that we should use his method. We decided to give it a test at noon: the result was mine was one twentieth of a mile out, while his was one and a half miles out... I don't think occasions like this have made me very popular with the Old Man.

Eventually they came to an agreement:

He has ceased trying to advise me on matters of navigation, but instead gives me hints on tanker practice.

The captain also had different opinions about the use of radar and on keeping time:

Instead of shifting the clocks on an hour every two or three days, this Old Man believes in shifting the clocks a few minutes each day, to keep time with the sun.

Nor was John impressed by the two stewards who stole his bin and didn't bring him his morning tea. He was however consoled by the possession of some of Barbara's underwear that she had left in his cabin by accident. He was also pleased that two swimming pools had been rigged up on deck. Barbara meanwhile was staying with her mother-in-law at John's brother's house in Ross on Wye and might have envied John his facilities on board ship:

Tonight, being Saturday, we have all had a good wash before going to bed. Mother was quite busy organising the pans of water! I'm sleeping in Mollie's bedroom now, so brought the small tin bath in here for my wash down.

John's mother told her more about John as a little boy:

If Michael has a mania for turning taps and running water, I shall know it is because of his Daddy, who could not be cured of that piece of mischief!

On the whole though, Barbara thought Michael had benefited from the week he had spent with his father. When she returned to Hull and her own parents, they commented on how well he had come on whilst away:

I said that was his Daddy's influence, for I am sure you made a great difference to him, darling, even if you did feed him chocolate biscuits.

She was very keen that Michael should learn his manners from an early age and that he should be set a good example:

For instance, if Daddy reads a book at meal-times, why should Michael be expected to put his comic down? Also, we ought to decide whether we are saying a grace at the beginning or end of each meal, as in six months' time, Michael will be ready to put his hands together, even if he cannot say anything, and have a grace said for him.

John replied:

Thanks for the reminder about reading at table. I shall have to be careful about such things. As for grace, I think it is a good idea to say it both before and after meals just as one says 'please' before you receive something and 'thank you' afterwards. If we just say it once at a meal I think it is best to say it before as you are all likely to be starting together but may not finish together, and it is the hardest thing in the world for a little boy to remain at the table after he has finished eating, without getting into mischief.

The British Guardian was heading again for Mena-al Ahmadi in Kuwait, where they would load cargo for Eva Peron in Argentina, so this put paid to any hopes of an early return to a UK port. However, each extra week away would entitle him to another 1½ days leave. At Port Said, hordes of peddlers again boarded the ship, before it sailed through Suez on the midnight convoy. As compensation for enduring the hot climate of the Red Sea, the officers and crew received an 'eastern bonus'. They were also given lime juice instead of coffee. The captain, however, insisted on full uniform being worn at meals.

'Strange Lady in Town' (Kuwait to Argentina)

Barbara was also enjoying very hot July weather and had decided that Michael need no longer wear a bodice. One day she decided to have a picnic lunch in Peter Pan Park with her mother, sister-in-law and their children:

> I wonder why sandwiches always taste so much nicer when eaten in the sun? We had a really lazy afternoon, the kiddies played on the sand, the babies slept, Mother read, and Joyce and I decided to have a swing. First, we went on the see-saw and had great fun. The only thing was Joyce being nearly two stone heavier than me nearly shot me off each time she went down. I wish we had a camera with us to record our return to childhood! After the see-saw we went on the big swing, and we were going quite high when some big boys came on. As they decided to take it really high, we decided to get off. Joyce was soon off, but I had more difficulty, as I was sitting with one leg at each side and could not get off until they stopped it. Boys being boys, at first they refused to bring the swing low enough and told me to 'jump for it'!

They also made the most of the heat-wave by joining a Sunday School outing to Bridlington:

> It was a glorious day, and we stayed on the beach until teatime. Mother had packed dinner for all of us. Michael thoroughly enjoyed it. After grovelling in the sand and grabbing Elaine's spade, he went paddling, first in a pool and then in the sea, and he could not have enough of it. The first time I got the skirt of my dress soaked, so the next time I took Michael down, I was wiser and tucked my dress in my pants! I could have done with a bathing costume – even the transparent one would have been useful. (I have just re-read the last few lines. I hope you do not think I tucked my dress inside my pants. I tucked it in the legs, like a romper suit.)

Another sunny afternoon they went to a garden party:

There was a Baby Show, so we decided to put the three little ones in it, whilst Madeleine went to see the Punch and Judy. It was the oddest of baby competitions, for although the doctor examined all the babies very thoroughly, by the time he came to give out the results, they had lost a lot of the cards, so the prize-giving was very haphazard. None of ours received a prize, despite the fact that everyone expected our Michael to walk away with first prize. Still, it was just one of those things. Michael was certainly very full of life and gave the doctor's nose a good pull when he was examining him.

Sometimes Barbara would leave Michael with her mother, taking over her job doing audience research for the BBC:

One man whom I interviewed said I ought to get a job as a TV announcer as I had the right sort of face and voice. I am still wondering whether he meant it as a compliment or insult, as his other remarks about TV had been rather disparaging.

Later in August Barbara and Michael spent a week with her sister and her children in North Norfolk, her brother-in-law being away in the army. She was impressed by the accommodation:

Today Joan has had workmen in most of the day, stripping up the old lino in the kitchen, and fitting new. The new lino is really good, and yet it is all absolutely free of charge. These married quarters really are very cheap – no wonder Percy does not mind being in the army.

They visited Wells-next-the Sea:

Wells is rather a pretty resort and the beach is backed by woods, so there is no promenade and it makes quite a change from the usual seaside town.

The sea at Wells was too far out for paddling, so they contented themselves with playing on the beach, but the next day they went to Blakeney Point:

The tide was out, which was just as well, as the sand was at the opposite side of the channel and we had to paddle across. When we went over, the water was only half way up my legs but coming back it came past my knees. The kiddies thought it was lovely.

Back home from her holiday, Barbara was thrilled to receive a telegram to say that John would be back in the UK at the end of September. She was also able to report that the presentation to John of his Silver Medal had been mentioned on the radio.

Heading meanwhile for Argentina via Cape Town, John needed to report the weather four times a day for the meteorological office in Cape Town. He had also received some more good news. For months he had been concerned that the collision near Finnart might count against his promotion chances, but he now found out that the solicitors for the Bjorn Clausen had admitted full responsibility. He was still busy mending his clothes, which were rather worse for wear after a year at sea:

When I come home you will find the pockets in my things all shapes and sizes. Whenever a hole appears I just fold it over the affected portion of the pocket or make a pleat, hence it feels like the catacombs when I am hunting in my pockets for something.

'I'll Come When you Call' (Argentina to the Isle of Grain)

At Eva Peron in Argentina, John handed out money to the crew and then went on cargo watch. He went ashore once with one whole pound to spend. There was little of it left after a haircut and contributing towards the cost of a football so that they could challenge the crews of other ships when in port. He also bought some shoes with American dollars for the equivalent of just less than three pounds. However, he had to go ashore a second time:

Just before we were due to sail from Eva Peron we had to check round to see everyone was on board and we discovered that about two thirds of the sailors were ashore at the nearest bar, along with a proportion of the staff of the other departments. Therefore, I had the job of going along to bring them back to the ship. After having a couple of drinks myself, I managed to shepherd about twenty of the crew back, all in various stages of inebriation. This finally left one fireman ashore and somehow or other he managed to get on board a tug and board us just as we were leaving the harbour.

When they were casting off, John had to manage without the A.B.s who were now unconscious, sleeping off their liquor. John was unimpressed by their behaviour:

In fact, we had quite a few fun and games at Eva Peron for we had as many of the crew going to see the doctor as a result of fights as we had due to other ailments. It makes me mad that the crew can go on like that in port, not doing one ounce of work and get away scot-free, for the Old Man, in spite of much strong talk, took no action against them.

John was also unimpressed by the captain's own attitude to work. With their return to the UK imminent, the British Guardian needed to be looking shipshape. The 'Old Man' had started painting the bridge on the ship but left the job for John and the Third Mate to continue once he 'started perspiring'. Barbara had expressed a concern that spending so much time in hot climates might have an adverse effect on John's fertility. John responded:

In view of your remarks, I have decided to spend the last fortnight before I reach home in the fridge, just to remedy the effect of the Persian Gulf weather.

Already, John and Barbara were thinking about a little brother or sister for Michael. There are no more letters from John in September, but he sent a telegram to say that they would reach the Isle of Grain in Kent on September 23rd.

Barbara was planning join John on board the ship. Eagerly she awaited a phone call from him via her neighbour, who always left the door open so that Barbara could go in if she heard the phone ring!

It would be two more years before John and Barbara had their own telephone.

Barbara took three week old Michael on board ship in Liverpool

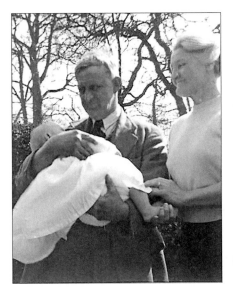

John's parents with Michael

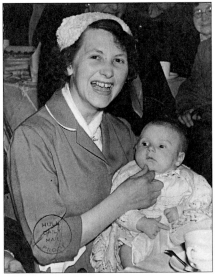

The youngest guest at the
American tea

Michael's christening

With Barbara's mother and Pip the dog

Hull officer wins silver medal

Highest marks in examination

From our Hull staff

The highest award for any Ministry of Transport examination—the Royal Society of Arts silver medal—has been awarded to a 26-year-old Hull man who is now serving as second officer on board the tanker British Guardian bound for Banias in Syria.

The officer, Mr. John Witty, of Westfield Road, Belgrave Drive, is

Second Officer J. Witty

not expected back home for two or three months. As soon as Mrs. Witty received word of the award for his work in the examination last year, she cabled to the British Guardian telling her husband.

A letter from the Royal Society of Arts stated that under the terms of the Thomas Gray Memorial Trust the Society offered a silver medal each year to the candidate who obtained the highest marks in the Ministry of Transport examination for the extra master's certificate. The presentation will be in London next November. It is the first time the medal has been won by a Hull man.

Mr. Witty started his career at the Hull Nautical School in 1941. By the time he left in 1944 he had been appointed Chief Officer at the school. For the next four years he served his apprenticeship with the Andrew Weir Shipping and Trading Company, and in 1948 he sat for his second mate's certificate. Two years later he took his first mate's certificate, passing it on his first attempt. In 1953 he took his master's certificate.

Barbara and Michael 1955

John at home with Michael, Autumn 1955

John shows Michael his silver medal

CHAPTER FIVE

COUNTING THE MONTHS: OCTOBER 1955 – JULY 1956

'Love Me or Leave Me'

Whilst on leave in the autumn of 1955, John made himself busy in the house. He decorated the bathroom, though it wouldn't be long before the damp came through again. He made a toy-box for Michael and decorated his bedroom ready for him moving into the big cot. Thinking ahead to Michael becoming more mobile, he made a gate to stop him getting into the veranda, and he patched up the leaky roof on the veranda.

John took Michael on a ride at Hull Fair and they spent a few days in London and at Ross-on-Wye, with John's brother. Barbara was feeling off-colour after having a miscarriage, but John put on some much-needed weight. Later he wrote:

There was no wonder I put weight on while I was at home for I was so contented. Although I enjoyed the nights when we went out together it was nice pottering around, doing things in the house, knowing you were there.

He was presented with his silver medal by the RSA and was again in the local papers.

They had an early Christmas Day. Barbara baked mince pies and they exchanged Christmas presents. Barbara gave John a wallet and Michael gave him a change purse. John bought Barbara a sewing machine. She wrote:

I often wonder how I managed to get my sewing done before I had my lovely machine. It certainly has saved me a lot of hand-sewing, and every time I use it, I feel grateful to you for giving me it, darling. You certainly gave me the most useful present possible.

Just before John left, he bought a vacuum cleaner to make the housework easier. Barbara later wrote:

> From being frightened of the hoover, Michael has gone to the opposite extreme and sits in front of the thing, waiting for me to brush him up. He thinks it is a grand game, but it makes it a much longer job. Still I do not mind, and I suppose the novelty will soon wear off.

On December 11th it was time to part again. Barbara was wearing a hat trimmed with roses as she said goodbye to John at Hull Paragon Station:

> When my hat fell off as the train was pulling out, I must have lost one of the roses.

'When You Lose the One You Love' (Falmouth)

It would be nine months before John would again be eligible for long leave. Little did they know that he would not be home again for eighteen months. John was heading for Falmouth overnight via Kings Cross, Paddington, Bristol and Plymouth. He wrote his first letter to Barbara whilst still on the train:

> At Hull there was just one man in the compartment and neither he nor I were in a talkative mood. However, he got off at Doncaster and another man got in. This man had apparently just been to see his father who appeared to be a bit of a religious crank. He had been arguing about this with his father and seemed to want to get it off his chest, for although I didn't encourage him in any way, he kept telling me about his arguments. My mind was far from thinking seriously about a subject like that last night.

The next leg of the journey also proved rather stressful:

> At King's Cross I got a porter to take my luggage to the 9.50 train whilst I went along to procure a seat. Having left my bag on a seat, I went to see if my luggage had been stowed all right. It didn't appear to be in either van, so I waited a bit and then had another look. Still no sign of the luggage, so I began hunting over the station and as a last resort glanced in the luggage van of the 9.45 which was leaving from another platform. There was my luggage! But even as I saw it, the train pulled out. I was relieved to find the 9.45 was also bound for Bristol and Plymouth and I just had time to shout to the guard to

put the luggage out at Bristol before I had to return to my own train for my bag, as it was about due to go.

Of course, all the time on the train to Bristol, I was visualising my luggage going astray, but at Bristol the other train was in. However, my luck was out, for the train moved off even as I approached it – and there was no sign of the luggage. I did however have time to remind the guard about it, and as the train moved into Plymouth, there was my luggage safe and sound on the platform. The excitement however was not at an end, for having packed the luggage into the Truro train and obtained a comfortable seat, I was only to find the part of the train I had got onto was going no further, so I transferred hurriedly again.

At Falmouth he joined the BTC Super-tanker SS British Talent as Second Officer. His cabin on board had a bigger bed, a settee, wardrobe, ensuite bathroom and toilet. If only Barbara could have joined him for a few days at Falmouth! Their departure was delayed at first because they had difficulty getting a crew together. In the end they would have to sail with five sailors short. Although this was John and Barbara's second Christmas apart since they got married, most seamen on leave wanted to spend Christmas at home. Barbara's trawlerman brother, John, also had no choice about working Christmas:

The ship's husband – I think that is what he is called – has threatened to sack anyone who takes a trip off to stay at home for Christmas. He has charge of all the Kingston trawlers, so it would be difficult getting a ship.

In fact, Barbara's brother was to have an accident on this trip, falling through the hatch into the fish room below deck, resulting in a cut to his head and some bruising. Meanwhile Michael seemed to be missing his Daddy:

Both on the bus and when we got home, he kept shouting 'Dad-dad' and waving his hand. Each time one of us opened a door, he would look up and say 'Dad-dad', and at tea-time he kept calling for you, as if he could not understand why you were not there.

I was quite certain you would phone tonight, and I was quite prepared for Mrs Dixon's tap on the window, I was through the door and over the little hedge like a streak of lightning. Have I ever told you darling that the sound of your voice over the phone sets me all a-tingling? I wonder what you will be doing the rest of the evening.

The departure of the British Talent was further delayed by the need for repairs, and it was frustrating to think that they could have spent these few days together on the ship. On December 15th, Barbara wrote:

If you could have seen me a few minutes ago you would have probably thought me the most dejected creature you had ever seen. I don't think I have ever felt quite so miserable. It seemed so wrong that we are parted when we could have been together. I am very sorry, my dearest, that I spoilt our phone call. I am afraid that I am not making things very easy for you.

John explained:

You will see how our sailing has been hanging fire all week, always scheduled for the next day. This is why I have been telling you not to come down – not because I didn't want to see you – for I am longing to see you again and hold you in my arms – but because each time it has appeared that you would no sooner get down than the ship would sail, and we should have the sorrow of parting again. Next time I join a ship, I think you had better come down with me and risk the ship sailing the next day. The trouble is that Falmouth is so far from Hull and so inaccessible.

Barbara wrote:

If only there was a really quick way of getting to Falmouth I think I would have come and risked you being annoyed with me. I would give anything just to be with you for an hour or so. But I suppose it is no use wishing for the impossible. It is only because I love you that I want to be with you every possible moment, but I realise it is not always as easy as that. I think I shall feel happier when I know that you have sailed because then I can start counting the days until you come back.

She was finding it hard to concentrate on domestic tasks:

I had mixed a caramel pudding, ready for adding the milk, and whilst the milk was on I decided to drain the peas, but instead of emptying them into the colander I tipped them all into the caramel mixture.

John meanwhile was cheering himself up by visiting Falmouth's pubs with the Mate. They went to the Riviera, the Albion and the Chain Locker:

It may appear that I have been pub-crawling every night – but I don't think it has been quite as bad as that, for intake has varied between only one and three pints a night, although even that makes the outing dear.

The ship finally sailed on December 18th. John sent a telegram to Barbara to let her know. It was clear from the beginning that John was unimpressed by the captain of the SS British Talent, describing him as 'rather a dry old stick'. He was scathing about his abilities as a navigator:

I have to be on the bridge in the morning to take a longitude sight and at noon to take a latitude and find the ship's position. I don't think this captain takes any altitudes to find the ship's position.

He was hoping Barbara would send more photographs of Michael, as he had altered so much since he had last been at sea. Michael was now quite a handful, finding he could reach up and grab objects on the table and on the draining board. He had just cut his second tooth. He was also taking an active part in Christmas shopping, especially as prams were not allowed in the department stores:

In Hammonds we were looking at some sets of cufflinks and tie-pins in boxes, and as we turned away, I noticed Michael was holding a box in his hand. I felt rather embarrassed as I put it back, but Michael was enjoying himself, and after trying to grab two or three ladies' hats as they passed by, he took mine and put it on his own head, causing a great deal of amusement to the crowd of shoppers.

At the same time, John was also having hat issues: his new uniform hat had blown over the side of the ship. Barbara decided Michael needed a hat of his own:

I bought Michael a little white helmet, to wear on windy and frosty days in the little pram. He looks very bonny in it, but quite different. Michael is all right until he remembers it and then he pulls it off.

Potty training was advancing very slowly:

Mother suggested putting it so that he could see it, so that he would go to it when he wanted it, but Michael thinks it is something to play with. Today he has glided it along the floors, put it on the chairs and settee, and put his face in it, but that is all.

After her miscarriage, Barbara had been hoping that she might again be expecting Peter or Shirley by the time John left. However, this was not to be:

Mother seemed to think that it is perhaps for the best that I am not pregnant again. She said I ought to concentrate on building myself up again during the next few weeks. I think your mother is of the same opinion – but I should have liked another little baby.

Barbara and her mother-in-law wrote to each other between visits:

I notice that in the last two letters she has sent me, they have been signed 'Dad and Mum', so I wonder if it is a bit of a hint that that is what she would like me to call her.

John replied:

Mother and Dad usually sign my letters 'Dad and Mum', but I stick to Mother, so you can please yourself.

The weather in Hull had turned very cold:

I washed this morning, and despite the frost decided to hang some towels out. Within half an hour they were stiff as boards. I left them out all day, but it did not thaw at all and at teatime I had difficulty in bending them to get them through the door.

'Ain't That a Shame' (Falmouth to Aden)

John had sent her a telegram to say that he would be calling at a British port at the end of January, but Barbara misinterpreted the code:

For twenty-four hours my hopes were very high, for I delightedly read it as the 27th 'instant'. All I could think was that your engines had broken down and you were coming in for further repairs. Whilst I waited for your second telegram giving me the port, I half packed my case and put all the clothes ready for packing. Then yesterday morning it occurred to me that it was possible you meant 27th January, so I rang through to London to make sure. Of course, I was told (by a charming man) that you would be going to either Finnart or the Isle of Grain at the end of January. I think it must be because I am wanting you so much that I jumped to the idea that it was this month when I should be with you again, for if I had given the matter proper thought I would have realised you meant next month.

In fact, John was already in the Mediterranean, cruising off the coast of North Africa, on the way to Mena-al-Ahmadi in Kuwait. The British Talent, built in 1952, was much bigger and faster than any other ship he had sailed on. It was a rather subdued Christmas on board ship:

I am afraid nobody on board seems full of the Christmas spirit. I think the majority of us are thinking of what might have happened if we had had our leaves extended another fortnight. We had a very nice Christmas dinner and although we had lots of courses I am sure I enjoyed the Christmas dinner we had together a lot more. This Christmas I have been strongly aware that there was something missing from the festivities, namely you. I wouldn't have minded how humbly we had to celebrate Christmas if only I could have been with you and Michael. This afternoon we had beer and a get-together in the smoke-room, but although I made myself sociable I am afraid my mind was too occupied in thinking of you to take a lot of interest in the songs and jokes.

He was looking through his photographs:

I realise I haven't had a full length one of you since we got married. Of course, it is rather cold to pose for a photo in your swimsuit, but all photos of you would be equally welcome.

Barbara spent Christmas day with her in laws this year. She wrote:

I must tell you this darling – more advice from your Dad. Michael had been absolutely full of mischief all day, climbing all over, sitting in the fireplace etc. We had been laughing at him, and then Dad said that we should have to be careful, as we could not do with a dozen like Michael. Then 'If you have another one like him, you had better call it a day, and not have any more.'

The next morning her mother-in-law brought her a cup of tea in bed and took Michael downstairs:

I thought of the other times when we had been there together, and that had been a signal for us to have a last cuddle together before getting up.

December 28th was their second wedding anniversary and John sent a telegram and flowers. He wrote:

It was certainly my lucky day when I married you two years ago, for no other girl could have done so much for me or meant so much to me as you do.

Barbara was delighted with the flowers:

The chrysanthemums are beautiful pinky-bronze blooms, and the daffodils are a real breath of spring. All my thoughts have been going back to what we were doing two years ago, and also to how I looked and felt last year. Little did I think that by this year we should have a young son who can climb onto almost anything.

She was a little anxious about what safety measures they could put in place when they visited the ship:

Have you found a long piece of rope to act as a 'baby chain' to make sure Michael does not go on deck? He can climb over most things and the steps would be no hindrance to him.

John was 'head over heels in work':

In addition to the usual chart-correcting and general maintenance, I have both store lists and inventories to complete before we reach Mena. Now to cap it all, we have six-hour watches (six on, six off). A little coaster is the cause for this, for it signalled us in the Red Sea and asked for a tow to Aden as its engines had broken down. At 11 pm I took our motor boat across to him with a line. Just after 4 am, when we were getting underway again, the tow-rope parted so I had the job again of taking it across.

By the way, this bit of towing comes under salvage, so we should get a little money for it. However, the ship is less than 200 tons, so it won't be much. The company will get most of the salvage money as compensation for the delay of the ship and the risk involved. Of course, to earn anything at all we have to reach Aden with our tow intact.

He was now seriously considering a switch to teaching:

It would appear that the grants are likely to be quite good. However, if you accept the grant you must stick to teaching and teaching alone. Looking at it that way, there are not big fields for advancement, but teaching certainly has its advantages as a career even though the pay is not too good.

New Year was celebrated more quietly than usual on board ship:

On these watches we couldn't afford to miss the sleep that attending a party would necessitate.

He was relieved to let go of the tow, especially as the wind started to come up after Aden:

Of course, all kinds of reports have to go in to London about this tow, but I noticed the Captain commended the small part I took, in getting connected and towing, so he must be quite satisfied with my work.

John seemed to be enjoying better relations with the 'Old Man':

He usually has the Chief and Second Engineers, the Mate and myself up for a drink each Sunday morning. In the Saloon however, I am not at the Old Man's table but sit with the Third Mate, Sparks etc.

He was no longer snowed under with work:

Having a little time on my hands during the past few days, I have indulged in sporadic bird-watching. There have not been many specimens to choose from though, and with a ship of this length it is difficult to observe the birds around the stern and this is where most of them congregate.

'Sandman' (Aden to Finnart)

As they came alongside at Aden, John was recognised by the Mate of the tug:

He sang out to ask me how my 'Harbour Light' was. He was one of the chaps who sat for Master at the same time as I did and of course he saw the article in the paper.

While berthed at Aden, John decided to take a walk across reclaimed land to the nearest village, about three miles away:

At first sight I appeared to be walking on fine white sand, but on examining it closer it was found to consist of myriads of tiny, exquisitely wrought white shells. Some were dainty spirals, others circular, whilst others had delicate spicules and prominences. On the left of the road the sea lapped gently at the beach while further out little black and white striped tropical fish darted in and out of the piles supporting the quay.

I had a stroll round the European quarters and I noticed most of their houses were of aluminium, something after the style of prefabs. Each had a small garden consisting purely and simply of sand. However, by constant watering and great perseverance, some of the occupants had managed to decorate their gardens with colourful flowers, which somehow managed to draw nourishment from the sandy soil. The gardens of some of the more enterprising occupants were a pleasure to the eye, whilst the less keen gardeners still managed to cultivate cacti amidst the sand and stones.

Most of the native workers live in large communal quarters, but an increasing number of rows of pleasant-looking white houses were going up for them and their families. In fact, one hill, which must have been the best part of a thousand feet high, was being rapidly blasted away to provide building stone. The houses and buildings stand out against a background of dun-coloured sand and rust-streaked mountains – some of the latter having been worn by the weather, sea and sand until their outlines have taken on all kinds of rugged, jagged and sometimes fantastic shapes.

At the end of the letter that John sent from Aden, he sent a row of kisses to 'Master one-year-old Michael'. As a postscript, he added:

I have enclosed a letter for Michael to tear up while you are reading this.

He was disappointed to get a change of orders which meant that he would not be visiting a UK port until February. He thought of Barbara enduring a cold January back home:

I wish I could give you a little of this weather or better still bring you here to enjoy it with me, but I wish… I wish… I wish… There are so many things I should like to happen, but foremost of those I should like to be with you. Anyhow perhaps another three weeks and we shall be together – if only for a day.

Barbara too was frustrated at the time lapse in their communications:

It seems so unfair that you do not learn about all Michael's achievements until weeks afterwards. I wonder how many times a day I start wishing you were here – several dozens I should say. I would not mind how poor we were, if only we could be together, for I am sure our love for each other would help us over all difficulties. On the other hand, I want you to do the work in which you can feel really happy, and I'm not too sure about teaching being the solution.

John was now enjoying life on the British Talent and pleased that over £3 was added to his wages for serving on such a large ship:

Now that I have got settled down on this ship, I am not finding the work particularly hard and I seem to have far more time than on a smaller ship.

Despite his qualifications, however, there were limited opportunities for promotion within BTC:

To obtain command before seeking a position ashore would mean a wait of from 8 to 10 years, at least in this company – a prospect which I think is out of the question.

The weather in England continued to be cold and snowy. When John telegraphed Barbara to tell her that he would definitely be calling at Finnart, on the west coast of Scotland, he advised her to leave Michael with her parents. Barbara agreed:

I think your suggestion that I do not bring Michael is a wise one, but I am sure it must have taken a lot of thinking about, for I know you will be longing to see out precious little son once more. I certainly feel it might be asking for trouble to take Michael such a long distance in this weather, as the contrast between inside the trains and waiting in the open is too great for such a little one. It is not as though he would be wrapped up snug in a carrycot – our young 'Mick' will not keep mittens on, nor his helmet, and frequently manages to slip out of his leggings!

As you will not be seeing Michael, I will let you into our secret, which was to have been a surprise. Michael had his first haircut on Wednesday and now looks really boyish.

'Love is the Tender Trap' (Finnart to Tenerife)

After just one night together with John on the ship at Finnart, Barbara travelled as far as Glasgow with the Chief Steward's wife:

I wondered if my feelings were showing when she said it is a heartbreaking life being married to a man who goes to sea.

Back home, the weather worsened further until there was over a foot of snow. The guttering was pulling away from the wall of the house under the weight of snow, but there was nothing to do but wait for the thaw:

I do not think that I have ever known such a long spell of this weather, and still there is no forecast of it ending. I could do with a sleigh for Michael instead of a pram. What does it feel like to be in a warm climate darling? I wish you could send me some warmth through the post, as it is bitterly cold again tonight and this coal does not seem to warm the room. I am almost shivering and there has been a good fire all day.

She was cheered up by a bouquet of irises, tulips and daffodils from John:

Receiving flowers when it is not an anniversary of any kind seems to give extra pleasure, and my lovely flowers have made me very happy.

She dreamt that John was visiting South America:

But the impossible happened in my dream, for Michael and I came out to see you on the ship. The scenery was really beautiful – it was in colour, so I must have had a technicolour dream. I felt quite 'glowy' when I woke up, until I realised you were not with me after all.

Whilst John had been on leave in the autumn of 1955, they had bought a number of things for the house, in addition to the vacuum cleaner. One of these was a pastry board:

I am beginning to think that the pastry board was worth every penny, for I am sure my pastry has improved greatly since we got it. I do hope that I can continue to improve, so that by the time you come home again I can produce first class pastry and no more 'punishment' cakes.

She had just done some baking:

The jam tarts are lovely, although I say it myself. Would you like one, my darling? I think it would be a little stale by the time you received it.

She was hoping that John would not lose so much weight on this trip, without her cooking to fatten him up. John replied:

I don't think I am losing weight just now, but in the summer out here most of us lose weight and then put it on when it starts getting cooler. There is no doubt that staying at home does me good (in many ways) and if I was at home all the time I should probably weigh about 17 stone.

He still had a year to fulfil on his current contract with BTC so there was little chance of him being home for good, for a while at least. Meanwhile, Barbara was finding Michael to be a handful:

He has been full of high spirits (and devilment) all day. He has tipped custard all over the floor, knocked over the draining board, tickled strange ladies on their necks (on the bus) and when we were in Fields this afternoon, he shouted to everyone until they spoke to him. I was glad to see him fast asleep in his cot and hope he stays that way all night.

The previous night he had woken up both sets of neighbours with his shouting and laughing. Barbara decided he needed his Daddy to settle him. John replied:

Michael certainly does seem adventurous, but he doesn't seem reckless and he goes very carefully about something new. You will need to be firm with him when he is in a naughty mood, but he does have such a disarming smile.

'Only You and You Alone'

Barbara also missed John's skills as a handyman:

The house seems to be dropping to pieces, for today the veranda door came off its top hinge, and it seems as if the damp has rotted away the door support. If you were home you could replace the wood, as you did elsewhere last time you were home.

The wallpaper in the bathroom was also suffering the effects of damp. Barbara suggested that John could paint it instead, when he came home on leave in the summer:

We could have the bath, toilet seat and cover, doors, skirting and window paintwork all the same green as now, and have the walls pale blue. I will strip the bathroom paper off, when your leave gets near, to save time when you are home.

John replied:

If we paint the bathroom green and blue, I shall probably think I am still at sea when bathing. It should look all right though, providing the blue is not too dark and tones in with the green.

On the ship, he was busy mending his radio and adjusting the ship's gyroscope. When it stopped working, a maintenance engineer came on board and tried to fix it, but in the end, John traced the fault to a bare wire in the centre of a coil. He was now trying to improve its accuracy and efficiency. A new captain had taken over the ship at Finnart:

> This Old Man seems a little bit finicky about small things. Apart from this characteristic however he seems all right, although another failing is an inability to admit when he is wrong. He doesn't seem to take a great part in the navigation of the ship and although he has been going to take altitudes of stars on various occasions, he has never got down to it. He seems to believe in going much closer to the various coasts than the last master did.

He had visited John's cabin on his regular Sunday inspection:

> He noticed the colour photograph of you and remarked that it didn't really do you justice.

Barbara was surprised that he had registered her appearance on her short visit to the ship. John replied:

> You seem surprised that the new Captain noticed what you look like, but you should know most sailors have an eye for a pretty face! However, to me no other girl's face is quite as pretty as yours, no other figure quite as trim, and certainly no one as dear to me as you (no pun intended).

Did Barbara take the hint about her spending? In March she wrote:

> I hope you do not disapprove too strongly, Darling, but I have bought another, more lightweight, folding pram for Michael. It cost £2.15.0, which I know is quite a lot considering we have one folding pram. But I have felt lately that struggling with Michael and the pram on and off buses is just too much. Although I feel I have done the right thing, I hope you do not think I am being unnecessarily extravagant, darling. Certainly, I could not manage the big folder if I was 'expecting' again. And now your very worried wife will say Goodnight and, trembling with fear, await her beloved one's comments.

John, however, had been on his own spending spree:

> I am afraid I have been rather extravagant during the past few days. Firstly, I bought myself a watch. I had been thinking of buying something about £2 to £5, but this one cost £6-2-0. It seems to be going very well though and has a guarantee, but it is still a lot of money. I hope you do not disapprove of my purchase. The other costly item concerns two courses of study with the College of the Sea. They advised me to start studying Pure and Applied Mathematics

if I considered taking a degree in the future. The fee is £1 per subject for enrolment and 5/- a year afterwards, which I think is quite reasonable. I have also written to the University of London to see whether I can be excused any of the entrance requirements. It rather looks as if I shall have to take the General Certificate of Education in five subjects before I shall be eligible to study for a degree. I think English, Geography and Physics will be the best subjects for me to take at ordinary level, and Pure and Applied Maths at advanced level.

He was wondering if he could swot up in time to take the GCEs in November. To his relief, the University of London said that he would be exempt from the minimum requirements, so would only need to take the Advanced Level exams.

Barbara took Michael and his new folding pram on the bus to visit John's parents in Beverley. Her father-in-law was a man with distinctive views about religion and worship:

Dad went to the Minster last night, for the 'very last time'. He does not know what church he is going to use in the future but has definitely finished with the Minster. I expect you will be hearing all the details shortly!

Her mother-in-law had wrapped the hot water bottle in John's old pyjama jacket:

I put it on over my nighty and pretended I was in your arms. I do hope you will return to the UK after your next trip to Aden, in which case it will be just under five weeks to when we are together.

She was hoping that he would visit the UK around the 20th April and then make a six-week trip so that he would be back again for his birthday:

I am waiting for your next telegram and hoping it will be 'Land's End for Orders'.

Imagine her disappointment when the telegram said that he would be going to the Canary Islands instead. John wrote in his letter:

I am afraid the blow fell the other day when we learnt that we shall be going back to Mena and then to Tenerife. Now it rather looks as if we won't be home until the end of May. It sounds rather as if Tenerife is the South American port you dreamed about, as it is a Spanish possession and very like the South American ports. It is actually an extinct volcano and the land is mostly mountainous and covered only by a few cacti and stunted shrubs. However, in the town of Santa Cruz where this ship berths there are many flowering shrubs, strongly scented and just one mass of colour when in flower.

'Memories are Made of This' (Canary Islands to Aden)

Although Barbara would not see the flowers of Tenerife, John sent her a bouquet of daffodils, tulips and freesia on the anniversary of their first meeting. He wrote:

I expect your thoughts as well as mine are drifting back three years ago to a certain dance at the Mission. After that dance, my life was never quite the same again. It became fuller and richer and much more contented. I think I treasure this day more than any other of the year, for if I had not met you on that Friday evening, none of the other wonderful times we have had together could have been fulfilled. I can hardly believe that, had one of us not gone to that dance, our lives might never have crossed. You are just the girl I had been waiting for – I hope I didn't disappoint you, for you were everything I had ever longed and hoped for.

Barbara was thrilled with the flowers:

They were a lovely surprise, for although I was thinking of you especially, I did not expect such a lovely present from you. It seems to me that I have known and loved you for much more than three years, but they certainly have been the happiest years in my life.

The winter was finally over, and crocuses were starting to flower in the garden:

They are all admired daily by Michael. He seems exceptionally observant for his age and will point out anything new.

Michael's speech was also progressing:

His latest is 'Oh dear me'. He says this if he sneezes, or trips. When he coughs, or pretends to, he puts his hand in front of his mouth with such an air of refinement. He really is amusing to watch, as he imitates what he has seen others do. Unfortunately, some of the phrases he is picking up from other people are not what I want him to say. 'Get out', 'Shut up' and 'Take that' are all phrases I would prefer him not to use. When he kisses, he opens his mouth

wide as though he is going to swallow me and is most passionate at times!
Sometimes he reminds me very much of you, Darling.

She added:

Have you ever heard the request programme for men on ships, on the
Luxembourg programme about 6.30 on a Saturday? I heard it for the first
time tonight and there was a request for someone on the British Hero. If you
do get that programme regularly, let me know and I will send in a request for
you, darling.

John replied that they didn't hear much of Radio Luxembourg at sea. He
mainly listened to the BBC Light programme during the day, and the BBC
Home programme in the evening. However, he was again spending his spare
time reading:

Yesterday I was looking at a book explaining the contents of the Koran and
I found it quite interesting. They ascribe to Christ only the role of a prophet,
but the rest of it is very similar to parts of the Old Testament. Its basic creed
is extremely simple, there being no Holy Trinity to explain about as in
Christianity and Hinduism. As a religion it also permits self-defence, which
Christianity does not.

He was now planning to come ashore after the expiry of his current two-year
contract with BTC in 1957, and then to take a BSc correspondence course in
Mathematics, whilst doing a temporary job:

I think a BSc in Physics is more valuable than one in Mathematics, but
without attending a university I should be unable to carry out the practical
side of the course. If I stay at sea, I am at rather a disadvantage studying, as
books of reference are not as handy, and also as a Mate I should not have a lot
of time. What is more important, I should be separated from you, and your
company more than makes up for the loss of wages and other advantages of
being at sea.

He had already started studying Maths, after a fashion:

I had the Electrician and the 2ⁿᵈ Engineer in my room after I came off watch
last night. They came in ostensibly to check on a mathematics problem, but
actually I think they were rather thirsty and neither had any beer in his room.

He was amused to read Barbara's account of Michael's latest antics:

Yesterday morning I got him ready to go out, except for coat and leggings, then built up the fire. When I went for the second shovel-full of coal, Michael had disappeared out of the veranda and had crawled through the front opening into the coal box. To say he was black is an understatement.

Michael was fascinated by watching the birds carrying twigs in their beaks to build their nests in the roof of the veranda. John was also bird-watching:

It helps to make the watches more interesting, for although the scenery doesn't change, the types of birds frequenting these coats seem to alter each month.

Near Tenerife, a white heron circled the ship several times. It reminded John of when he and Barbara had taken his parents to see 'The Flight of the White Heron' at the cinema, although that had actually been a film about the Queen's tour of the Commonwealth. On the way to Aden, a pelican landed on the ship:

For several hours there were several bird-watchers, also quite a few attempts to catch it. Tim, one of the apprentices, bought a canary at Tenerife. It was a nice bright yellow then, but since then it has gradually got darker and darker and now looks much more like a sparrow than a canary. Its song doesn't differ from a sparrow's either!

The ship was now sailing back and forth between Little Aden and Mena-al-Ahmadi, and John was finding it somewhat monotonous:

The trouble with this Mina-Aden run is that it seems to be one long sea trip with extra work every five or six days, for there is practically nothing ashore at either end. The only thing that makes it bearable are the letters we receive at each port.

'See you later, Alligator' (Aden to Kuwait and back)

As soon as they received orders for home, he would be ready to put in his request for leave. He reckoned that it would be around June 22nd, by which time he would be due five or six weeks of leave. Already John and Barbara were making plans for how they would spend his summer leave: in addition to catching up on household repairs, they would have a few days at the seaside.

For the time being they were making do with photographs. John wrote:

The photo of Mother, Dad and Michael is quite good, but Michael looks a little too much of an angel in it. How about some photos of you (preferably in a bikini)?

Barbara replied:

Bikinis are old fashioned now, darling, but I will bring a bathing costume down to the ship next time, so you can take a snap of me wearing it.

John was looking ahead to his summer leave and was concerned that it should not be completely taken up with decorating. He gave Barbara instructions on how she could make a head start with decorating the bathroom:

You could get all the old paper stripped off and if there was still a good bit of time before I came home you could try distempering the ceiling. The walls will need a coat of flat paint before applying the enamel, and the flat paint (undercoat) should either be white or a slightly paler shade of the final colour. There are also one or two small holes to be plastered up with some of the alabastine we have in the corner by the fuses. If you use a roller the main thing is to see that all the paint is cleaned off the roller each time you knock off work (this is done with paraffin or such like). To use a roller economically, all the painting of the one colour should be done at the same time, otherwise a lot of paint is wasted each time the roller is washed out. Also, I should make sure that the whole of the floor, bath etc, is covered with old newspaper.

Meanwhile, Barbara had been asked if she could do a few days' work at Northern Dairies. She had kept in touch in case she needed a job when John came ashore. John's parents agreed to come over to look after Michael. She found it strange to be back at the desk where she had written many of her first letters to John:

I was quite surprised at the warm welcome I got from everyone, and it has been made clear that I would be welcomed with open arms if I wanted to come back full-time. But, unless it was necessary, I prefer to be just a wife and mother. I do not know why I said 'just', for they are the two most important things to me. I only wish I was able to be a proper wife all the time.

She did however find the company stimulating:

Apart from the work, I have had discussions on religion, government, foreign affairs, and the advantages of electricity in the future, and I feel more mentally alert than I have done for some time.

And she wasn't tied to her desk all day:

This lunch-time, Reg Williams gave four of us a lift into town in his car, then after lunching at Hammonds Self-Service, he took us down to the pier for two minutes blow. I felt really love-sick for you, dearest. I think the sea will always be connected with you, in my mind.

John responded:

I think it is very much preferable for you not to go out working, but if I am switching from the sea to a shore job it may possibly be necessary until I get properly settled. I think it is far better for Michael if you can be home most of the time. You must spend your week's wages on something for yourself, for you will be needing things for the summer.

John was careful with his spending, having experienced the financial difficulties his parents suffered when the family business failed, and always made sure that a proportion of his salary was put aside for the future. In the April budget, the government introduced Premium Bonds. Barbara asked John what he thought of the idea. He replied:

I don't think much personally of the Premium Bonds idea and I am sure the incentive to save is in the wrong direction.

Although Barbara enjoyed shopping and spending money, she was also capable of economising:

Do you remember that old shirt of yours which we ripped last time you were home? I have used the back of it tonight to line a pair of trousers for Michael. It is ideal material for this purpose, so if you discard any white shirts whilst you are away, do not dump them, but bring them home, as I anticipate requiring plenty of trouser linings in the future.

She had been to an American Tea in aid of the Mission to Seamen:

It was a tremendous success – there must have been 150 there. I was hostess at one of Mother's tables. One of the main features was the new film on the work of the Mission. It was a story of how the Missions in different countries link up when necessary to help seamen and their families. It seemed extremely factual and, particularly when it showed the BP tankers at Little Aden, I felt extremely lonely for you, darling, and was glad it was dark!

At this time, John was anchored in a dust storm near Mena:

> *You might wonder at us having a dust storm at sea, but it is real enough and uncomfortable enough. The visibility is only about a quarter of a mile and dust and sand is everywhere. On the land I expect they are having a sand storm, but by the time the wind reaches us the heavier particles have dropped and just the dust remains. However, it is not the dust which stops us berthing but the wind which goes with it. This morning we dragged our anchor a quarter of a mile and since then we have dropped our other anchor to hold her in position. It is that dark that I can hardly see to write this letter, yet it is 11 am and at the height of summer. The sand has made the sky a yellowy colour although above the layer of sand I expect it is cloudless.*

'Lost John' (Aden to Greece)

Barbara's next few letters did not reach John immediately. On the envelopes is written in capital letters: ADDRESSEE NOT ON BOARD.

On June 8th, she wrote:

> *Tomorrow you are due to arrive at Aden, and still no telegram. I do not know what to think.*

With John expected home in a few weeks, she was trying to decide between Bridlington and Filey for their summer holiday. When a telegram finally arrived however, it was to say that John was not heading for home after all, but for Bombay. Nevertheless, she expected that he would be back by the end of July.

On June 12th she received a second telegram and she immediately responded:

> *Congratulations, sweetheart, on your promotion. I was thrilled to receive your telegram giving me the glad news. You certainly deserve the promotion, darling, and I am very, very proud of my Chief Officer. I shall now have to look up the list of tankers, which you sent me some time ago, and find out what sort of ship the Enterprise is. I wonder how you are settling down on her and what your fellow officers are like. Did you have a big rush to pack your things to transfer them? I do feel that now you have left the Talent I may see you sooner.*

On June 16th, John explained what had happened:

I didn't learn I was to be transferred to the British Enterprise until we arrived at Aden and then it was still not definite until an hour before she sailed, when I was rushed across with my luggage. The previous Mate was paying off sick and he left when I boarded so I had very little chance of learning anything from him. Hence, I have been head over heels in work for the past few days. A lot of the work had been allowed to drop a long way behind, so I am trying to get things up to date. As we are bound for Piraeus and Salonika in Greece I have a few days to get things sorted out but not long. Of course, very shortly the half-yearly inventories have to be filled in, so I shall have plenty of work on for another fortnight or a month.

I'm afraid this change has put rather a damper on my hopes of coming home soon, for she only left the UK at the beginning of May. She is only a small ship – about 8,000 tons – but quite big enough for me at the present. I am sending you a money order for £71-13-4, which is the balance of my wages from the Talent. On this ship I have increased the allotment to £60, but it is dated rather later so you will be about a month without an allotment.

Now I must be turning in as it is about 10 pm and I must be up again at 4. Once I settle down into a routine I shall have quite a lot of sleep to catch up on. With this new position I am afraid I won't be able to carry on with the Mathematics for a while, as I just haven't the time. These ships usually call at ports every few days too, so I shall be kept busy. Another snag about this ship is the lack of apprentices, which is quite keenly felt. Bosun seems quite good but the Carpenter and Pump-men aren't too special.

Bye-bye now my sweetheart. I love, love, love you and I shall never be too busy I can't find time to think of you.

'Zambezi' (Greece to Suez)

The Civil War had left Greece in ruins, the country was struggling economically and there was mass emigration. Barbara wrote:

I do hope there is no trouble in the part of Greece you go to, as it is not one of the nicest places at the moment, is it? I wonder whether you were able to buy any shirts at Piraeus or Thessalonica. I hope so as I should hate to think the British Enterprise had a raggy Chief Officer!

In fact, he had a rather trying time in Greece. As Chief Officer, John was responsible for the cargo:

We nearly mixed our cargo. The shore foreman came along and told me they were receiving Kerosene instead of Gas Oil, and I found the Chief Engineer had left a coupling connected which shouldn't have been. Of course, the Mate is supposed to check all the lines and had the cargo mixed I wouldn't have held this job for long. At Salonika we had a leak in the submerged pipeline to the shore and on one occasion they shut the wrong valve ashore, causing our pump to stall and also a number of leaks. Of course, these were out of our control, but nevertheless there is never a dull moment.

He was wondering whether he might be transferred back to the British Talent if they flew out a permanent Mate for the Enterprise:

In any case, I am hoping I shall not have to do the full time on this ship until she dry-docks next.

Barbara wrote:

I too am finding this long separation unbearable, and spend my time longing to be with you. Michael is good company though, bless him, and is becoming an extremely affectionate little boy. I think he realises I am missing you and in his little way tries to make up.

Michael would often distract her from the housework:

I was ironing this afternoon but kept breaking off to play with Michael and to dance with him. He says 'Dance with me' whenever any jazzy music comes on. You should see us dance to Zambezi!

It was now over six months since John had seen his son. The seventeen-month Michael could be both a joy and a handful:

It seems such a shame that you cannot see Michael growing up for he is altering so much now. He is such a mixture of roughness and loving, although usually he gives 'rough love'. For instance, if I am carrying him downstairs, he may suddenly decide to give me a big hug and kiss, and the sudden impact nearly knocks me off balance! Michael is a real darling though and I think he is getting to know that some things are just not to be done. For example, a bucket of water when I am scrubbing the floor must not be touched by Master Michael. The following happened this morning. While I was scrubbing the floor, he persisted in trying to either put things in the water or to grab the floor cloth. For the first two or three times I removed him firmly, said 'Don't touch – burn' and gave him his tins to play with. About the fourth time I just looked at him and said 'Michael', very sharply. He immediately moved back and said, 'Don't touch', so I asked him what Mummy did to little boys who were naughty, and he replied, retreating smartly, 'Smack bottom.' From then onwards I had no more bother from him! Considering it is only very occasionally he has had to have his bottom smacked, I think he is learning, don't you Darling? By the way, do you agree that for persistent naughtiness, a smack is the answer? If not, what do you suggest?

She was thinking about the miscarriage she had had in the autumn:

Our baby would have been due this week. I wonder what it would have been – a girl, I expect. Still, perhaps it was for the best. I do hope we start a second baby soon though, for Michael's sake, as not only does he need a playmate, but he is getting used to all the limelight, which is not a good thing.

She had just lost another tooth:

As this means I shall have a big gap at the right-hand side, please note that all future photographs of me will be serious ones. I can see Michael will soon have more teeth than his poor old mother! He seems to have quite a few coming through now, but I have not had an opportunity to check up yet – it is a dangerous job!

'I'll be Home' (Suez to Liverpool)

On July 1st, Barbara was thrilled to get a telegram to say that the Enterprise would be calling at 'Land's End for Orders' on July 25th:

There was no doubt that Michael understood what your telegram said, for his little face was wreathed in smiles, and he gave me a big hug just to show he was happy too. I do hope you will be as proud of our big boy as I am, when you see him, but you are sure to be. The only thing that bothers me at all, when we are on the ship with you, is that he can only sit still at the table for as long as he is eating, but I expect no one will mind if he has a trot around (I hope!!). I hope you have thought up plenty of safety precautions for our quiet, gentle, timorous little boy!

She continued:

> The 25th July cannot come quick enough for me, and now I shall get on with
> my sewing with much more interest. I doubt whether I shall manage to get
> all Michael's things done and a dress for myself, so I may buy one if I see
> something in the sales. I must not forget to buy a bathing costume too!

She was hoping that John's ship would be coming to a UK port:

> I wonder if you have applied for your leave or not? I have a feeling you may
> come back home with us but of course it may be wishful thinking.

John was struggling to find time to write but sent flowers to Barbara on July
9th. He explained in his next letter:

> The trip from Suez to Aden was just one mad rush around with inventories
> to make out, store lists to send in and damage and repair lists. Fortunately,
> the cargo we had to load did not call for the usual planning as it was to be
> all Kerosene. Well, I got the lists made up after a fashion and also planned
> where the cargo was to go. All this planning was in vain though, for when we
> arrived at Aden we were told right out of the blue that we were now to load
> two different types of oil, so I had to re-plan all the cargo. Whilst I was doing
> this, other things had to suffer, and I'm afraid letter-writing was one.
>
> Now the pressure of work has eased off a little, but how I am going to get the
> ship looking something like before we reach home I don't know. It is supposed
> to be painted from truck to keel, but at the present it looks like a rust-box,
> and there is the prospect of rough weather ahead.

He had some disappointing news for Barbara about his summer leave:

> I have not put in a leave letter as it would appear I was finding a Mate's job
> too much for me if I did. However, I wouldn't be surprised if I am relieved
> when we reach home and I am really hoping I shall be, as I am not looking
> forward to staying on this ship in the Mediterranean for the next six months.
> Of course, it will most likely mean going back Second Mate, but it would also
> mean I could get on with the Mathematics and my plans for leaving when
> this contract expires. If I stay on this ship, my plans are going to be rather
> dished up and this temporary promotion has not altered my previous plans.

On the 14th July he sent Barbara a telegram to say that he would be coming
to the Dingle Peninsula, near Liverpool. She was delighted as it was such an

easy port to travel to. It would be eighteen months since the last time she had made the journey, with a new-born baby:

> *I wonder whether you will be coming home with us, but if you do not, then I shall be hoping the British Enterprise makes short trips.*

Little did they expect that this visit to Liverpool would be the last time they saw each other for a full year.

CHAPTER SIX

A LONG SEPARATION: JULY 1956 – JULY 1957

'Heartbreak Hotel' (Liverpool to Suez)

After a couple of days together on the ship at Liverpool, John and Barbara were separated again. John wrote:

The two and a half days we had together last week seem to be almost a dream now, although a very pleasant dream while it lasted. I wonder how much of those days we had together? Just a few hours I expect. I am longing to be with you again and to have a little time just with you, for even Michael can be a nuisance at certain times!

Barbara agreed:

It was lovely being with you for a brief while, dearest, and even though we did not have much opportunity to be on our own, I was happy to know you were there. I think if you do make another trip home before your leave, we will have to transfer Michael to the settee when we go to bed. Gosh, wasn't he jealous! I can laugh now, but I did not think it funny at the time. There seemed so little time that we were together, and then if it wasn't Michael being jealous, it was the Third Mate walking in on us – what a life! Thank you once again my sweetheart for being so wonderfully good and kind to me. What a perfect husband I have. And I am sure Michael thinks you are the best Daddy in the world too (even though he may fight you for my attention!). His favourite remark is 'Where's Dada gone?'. I think he expects you to pop up from behind a chair, or something.

The next time John could be sure of returning to the UK would be in February when the ship was scheduled to dry-dock. By then his contract would be almost due to expire, so that he would be able to take his leave and set about looking for a shore job. On July 28th, Barbara wrote:

Three years ago, today (by the day), you met me at the Regal corner, after a four-month trip. How quickly things happened after that, yet all were happy things – and I for one shall always be glad that events did so happen. I remember that on the Westwood that afternoon, you asked me what I thought about marrying someone who was away for long spells, and I blithely answered that I expected one would get used to it. How little I knew, for I am certain now that I could never get used to you being away, as each time I leave you it seems far worse. But at least this time I have something tangible to look forward to, even though February is a long way away.

There was already a hint however that there might be problems ahead. Barbara wrote:

I am wondering whether the Suez situation will affect you or not. I suppose there is a possibility of you going right round by the Cape of Good Hope. I have just been listening to our neighbour's TV for the news, and I gather that all Royal Navy ships are to go round by the Cape. I am rather worried about what you will be doing, for I should not like your ship to get held up or anything.

She also mentioned that Army Reservists were being recalled, and that several people had asked her whether John was in the Suez area. On August 8th, she wrote:

I have the radio on as I do not want to miss Anthony Eden's speech. I wonder if you will be listening to it too, or are you too far away to get the BBC? He is on now, and I have been listening to him. So far, he has only explained the position in Suez. I wonder what the result of next week's conference will be. The public opinion at home seems to expect another war, although I think everyone hopes that it will not come to that.

A couple of days later, she wrote:

I read in tonight's paper that there is a threat to sabotage the Bahrain oil refinery. I cannot help wishing you were on any type of ship other than a tanker. Still, I must not start worrying, as it may all blow over easily.

A fortnight since they had parted at Liverpool, she had not yet received any letters or telegrams from John, who was on his way back to Piraeus and

Salonika in Greece. He warned her that it would be risky trying to send mail from Suez. The British Enterprise had just passed through the Suez Canal when John wrote:

> *Things appear to be quiet in the canal zone, but most people are wondering about its future.*

'Why do Fools Fall in Love?' (Suez to Aden)

There was to be no new baby after their brief time in Liverpool. Barbara wrote:

> *I do hope we manage to start one soon after you come home, as much for Michael's sake as anyone else's now. He really does love babies, and also, he needs a little playmate of his own. He calls his bedtime bunny 'my baby' and makes quite a performance of tucking it in.*

Barbara now had eight nieces, but no nephews. She was sewing a dress for one of her nieces:

> *I wish I were making a dress for our daughter – I wonder whether we shall have a girl, or just boys. Michael's clothes from now on will become more boyish. I think he has outgrown lace and embroidery, don't you, Darling?*

Whilst desperate to have her husband at home with her, Barbara was worried that she might have pressurised John into thinking about taking a job ashore:

> *Darling, are you really sure you want to leave the sea? For, as many have pointed out, you have worked so hard for your present position that it may be a shame to give it up. Perhaps I have been rather selfish in letting you know I miss you and constantly long to be with you, but dearest if you would rather stay at sea, I shall understand and just make the most of it. I shall always love you most of all whatever decision you make, and most of all I want you to be happy.*

Having missed out on the seaside holiday that she had planned to have with John, Barbara took Michael to Bridlington for a few days in August, staying at a flat that her mother had rented for a week. They were joined by her sister-in law, with her three small daughters:

> *You should have seen us when we got off the train: two adults, four children, two prams and four cases. No wonder the taxi driver would not take us!*

Although Michael started by flattening every sand pie that he saw, he soon got the hang of bucket and spade work, and he had his first ride on a donkey. The weather proved somewhat unpredictable:

> We had just settled down on the beach when there was a heavy thunderstorm. You can imagine what a time we had putting on macs, then getting two prams and four children onto the promenade and to a shelter. By the time we got there, it had stopped raining.

'Born to be with you' (Aden to Greece)

Despite enjoying their holiday, Barbara was glad to be back home:

> I have felt quite home-sick the last day or two. Even though you are not here, I feel much closer to you in our own home. Probably it is because we have shared so much happiness here. I hope we share much more in the not too distant future.

John was still sailing between Aden in Yemen, Port Said in Egypt, and the Greek ports, using the Suez Canal to pass from the Red Sea to the Mediterranean. Barbara was concerned at what she heard in the news:

> I wonder what will happen to Makarios now it has been discovered he is leader of the EOKA terrorists? What with Suez and Cyprus, you do seem to be coasting in the trouble spots, darling. I do hope you will be safe.

EOKA was a Greek nationalist guerrilla organisation campaigning for the end of British rule in Cyprus. Archbishop Makarios was a very popular figure among Greek Cypriots as he passionately supported the unification of Greece and Cyprus, but he denied any involvement in violent resistance. In 1956, Makarios was in exile but he later became president of Cyprus. John was, however, seeing a more peaceful side of Greece in the August of 1956, having been asked to accompany the Captain ashore:

> First, we had a walk along the main street at Salonika which is also the seafront and I found it quite enjoyable watching the crowds streaming by. Salonika is quite a large town and the shops in the town centre seemed modern and full of goods. By the way I bought myself a comb, having once more lost mine. Later we went to a cabaret bar and had a few beers there. There was no floor show on, but several girls were floating around the bar and trying to press their attentions on us. I went so far as to have a couple of

dances with them, but my mind was far away thinking of you and wishing I was dancing with you. I didn't enjoy the dancing or the company but at least it was a change. As such it was probably worthwhile, for chances to go ashore are few and far between.

Barbara replied:

You certainly did right to have an evening ashore, for you have had very little relaxation since joining this ship, and I'm sure the change of scenery (etc!) would do you good. It seems ages since we had an evening together, or for that matter, any time at all on our own.

She did not seem to envy John the companionship of the Captain, having met him at Liverpool. She wrote:

How is my friend the Captain – still as sarcastic as ever? Does he still call you 'Mr Ahem'?

'A Sweet Old-fashioned Girl' (Greece to Egypt)

On August 29th, Barbara was preoccupied:

I wonder whereabouts you are now, Darling, and whether your thoughts like mine have been on the day we got engaged, three years ago. I think I was so occupied in thinking of you, darling, that I failed to concentrate on my baking. Consequently, my sponge roll stuck to the tin, and I dropped the chocolate cake. Then to crown it all, the white sauce went lumpy, so I had to empty it out and start again. What it is to be lovesick!

Do you like fish pie, darling? I made one for dinner today, and it seemed to go down very well. That at least turned out successful. Also, do you like mushrooms? If you let me know some of your favourite dishes, I will practise making them while you are away.

John was struggling to keep on top of his jobs:

With these short trips, I seem to be getting very little done on the ship and each day it gets rustier and scruffier. At Alexandria I got part of the ship's side painted but it will be rusty again in a few weeks. I am still busy practically all day long and I have hardly had time to look at my Maths books, never mind doing any studying. I have just about caught up with writing up my Log Book but now the overtime sheets are way behindhand and there will be all kinds of disputes cropping up if I don't get them written up.

Today the 'Bumboat' was alongside at Port Said and I spent quite a bit. Among my purchases were two pairs of khaki shorts, a fountain pen and a pair of light shoes. I also bought several pairs of white socks and another airmail pad. The other day I did a big wash and I was just congratulating myself on getting some clean shirts at last, when I noticed that two pairs of my white shorts and two pairs of khaki shorts were torn and frayed at the edges. This necessitated the new purchases. I do not want to buy a lot of gear now though, for my requirements may be entirely different after March. After we had left Alexandria, I nearly had a fit, thinking my watch had been stolen. However, I had just put it in one of those safe places where even I couldn't find it.

A shortage of pilots meant that there was only one convoy a day through the Suez Canal. Barbara had picked up on this:

According to tonight's news, the non-Egyptian pilots are resigning at the weekend. I wonder how this will affect you. I can't help wishing you were safe at home with us. The unrest seems to be spreading throughout the world. Do you think there will be a war?

'Whatever Will Be Will Be' (Leaving the Middle East)

A telegram arrived for her on September 14th and she responded:

Although it would have been nicer if you had received orders for the UK, I was very relieved to hear you are going to Australia, out of the Suez area.

She was listening to the Last Night of the Proms on the radio:

Have I ever told you that one of my unrealised ambitions is to attend the Albert Hall for this last concert of the season? Still, I can enjoy it almost as much by listening and imagining. On the radio, 'Rule Britannia' is being sung, and the audience is joining in with extra feeling. Somehow it seems quite appropriate at the present time. I wonder how the Suez trouble will be solved.

She continued:

The 10pm news is now on, and it rather sounds as though Russia will join Egypt if there is any war, and I am afraid it beginning to look very much like war.

However, Michael's continuing antics provided comic relief from the worrying news:

Michael's latest expression is 'By Jove' and he tacks it on to nearly everything he says. It does sound comical. I am also beginning to think he has the makings of a first-rate shoplifter. Whilst we were in the toy department at Hammonds, I suddenly noticed he had a small ball in each hand, and we were well past the ball stand. Of course, I took them back and apologised profusely. When we are at Beverley, it seems that his one ambition is to hit the light shade with his ball, and no matter how often he is checked he just starts again. Then he puts Squeaky (the policeman-dog you bought him at Swansea last year) in his pram and rushes it up and down the hall regardless of anyone who may also be in the hall. I think your Dad is glad he only has him in small doses!

Now that John was on his way to Australia, it would be weeks before he received any letters, but Barbara continued to document her daily life. She had finally had her missing teeth replaced with dentures:

My new teeth fit quite comfortably, but I am still rather conscious of them. Yesterday I seemed to talk as though I had a mouth full of pudding, and food does not taste the same. Still, I suppose one must sacrifice something in aid of vanity!

She had encouraging news for John from the Merchant Navy Journal:

According to the principal examiner, 'there is still a shortage of men with this high qualification (Extra-Masters), both in the industry and in the teaching profession'. That being so, you ought to be able to take your pick of the best jobs.

'The Wayward Wind' (On the way to Australia)

John was certainly finding his current job rather trying. On September 26th, he wrote:

I thought the trip down to Australia would be easier as regards work, but an accident happened which rather altered matters. Soon after we left Aden we ran into a spell of bad weather and two of the hatches which I thought were securely battened down were leaking. A considerable amount of water entered the tanks and oil escaped from them, before we got them properly secured. When something like this happens to the cargo the company takes a dim view of it. As seeing the tanks are securely battened down is one of my responsibilities, I expect I shall hear more about this. Anyhow I can't see them putting me back to Second Mate until the end of the trip, and if not too much oil has been lost I may just get a black mark in the books. Since then I have been going round the other tank lids replacing them, as a repeat of this would certainly bring more than a black mark. Half the trouble is due to the lids having got bent through frequent tightening down. The other half is due to the Carpenter not having tightened the lids down sufficiently, although of course it is my direct responsibility. Another contributing factor lies in the packing, which was not brought high enough up when inserted, but here again I suppose I should have had it replaced.

Barbara received this letter on October 11th. She replied:

You certainly do seem to be unlucky on this ship, but it is a wonder more things do not happen, considering the long hours you work. I would much rather you shared your troubles with me, darling, for then I feel that although I cannot be a wife to you in some ways whilst you are away, at least I can share your tribulations!

John however would not receive this letter until he reached Adelaide on October 20th. In the meantime, he had other concerns:

At the present my worry is fresh water and whether we shall have enough on board to reach Kwinana. Due to persistent head winds, we are already two days behind schedule and when we are loaded we have a very narrow margin of fresh water on board. Already I have had to cut down some of the supplies.

Another worry was the condition of the ship. Built in 1946, the British Enterprise would be scrapped in 1961:

It is certainly a thankless job being Mate of a ship like this. I just don't seem to be able to keep pace with the rust on the paintwork, no matter what overtime the crew work. The ship just seems to go from bad to worse. This trip down from Aden when I had hoped to get some work done on the ship, spray has been blowing about continuously and there has hardly been a dry day on the decks. When a dry day does seem to come along, my plans seem to get upset by the weather changing again. Being two sailors short of the normal complement doesn't help any, and I am wondering how many more we may be short of when we leave Australia.

It looked at one point as if they would be another man down:

The other night I was woken up about two in the morning by a white-faced sailor who told me there was a man overboard. It was rather a wild night so searching for him wouldn't have been a picnic. As I was getting dressed I heard the engines stop and I was just about to go on the bridge when another sailor came in to tell me they had found the man fast asleep in another cabin. We had already launched a lifebuoy and turned the ship around, so it came as rather an anti-climax, but as a relief too.

He anticipated more drama when they reached Australia:

Generally, there is a good deal of drunkenness amongst crews on the Australian coast, so I expect I shall get still less work done on the ship in the next fortnight. It looks as if we shall be on the Australian coast whilst the Olympic Games are on – it is a pity we couldn't knock off work for a couple of days to go to see them.

'Singing the Blues' (Half a world away)

He was however looking forward to receiving some letters, as he was missing his wife and son:

It is only 2½ months since you were with me at Dingle, but somehow it seems much longer. I think I am looking forward to my next leave more than my previous one, for I have been away almost continuously since the beginning of December last – almost 10 months. Anyhow I am just looking forward to the end of January or beginning of February when I should be home again. It is said that the Chief Officer who preceded my appointment couldn't leave the ship quick enough and I shall be no exception. Of course, I wouldn't like to get the sack at the end of the trip, but I won't feel as if the bottom had dropped out of my world if I do. I hope you wouldn't feel too bad about it either. I certainly feel that there is no future for me in this company. Perhaps one of the reasons I have done nothing but moan in this letter is because I feel frustrated. Mainly frustrated with not being able to be with you and Michael, frustrated at not being able get on with the studying, and frustrated at not being able to get things done on the ship to improve matters.

Back home, Barbara was finding Michael's behaviour rather trying at times:

As the shops were very full, I left the pram at Hammonds, and His Lordship ran, walked and jumped as we went along. We had not been in the shop five minutes when Michael said 'Kick', and I turned to see an elegant lady rubbing her shin. When later on Michael said 'Jump', I half knew what to expect, and sure enough he had jumped on a gentleman's foot. But believe me, Darling, whilst I am apologising to one person, Michael is busy pushing someone else out of the way. When he is in one of those moods I do not seem to make any impression on him, no matter what I say or do. I think it is time he went to school!

Nevertheless, the toddler did have some more angelic moments. Barbara took him to a Harvest Festival service:

During each prayer, Michael put his hands together and said 'Gentle Jesus'. He is learning it quite well and says it along with me at bedtime now, although not all the words are very clear. 'Suffer me' is one phrase that he seems to say quite easily.

In the autumn she had the Hoover vacuum cleaner serviced, as they had now had it for a year. The Hoover representative then brought her a new Hoover all-electric washing machine to try out, 'without obligation':

The all-electric model is certainly a big improvement on the other washers I have seen, and it pumps out the water and refills within 3 minutes. I was rather amused at the representative, when we were discussing when he should collect the washer. He wanted to know when my husband would be in, presumably to try and press for a sale (at least I think that was the reason!), so I told him he would have a long wait.

In John's absence, Barbara got someone in to help decorate the sitting room. While they did the wallpapering, she tackled the paintwork:

I did it all very carefully, and I am pleased to say I made very little mess on the floor. Certainly, I did it very differently to the slap-happy way I painted the dining room two years ago. That was when I was expecting Michael. What a lot seems to have happened since then.

Michael continued to surprise her:

That son of ours astonished and amused me yesterday, for when I called him for dinner, he came marching in shouting 'Down with women, down with women'. I cannot think where he got it from.

He was learning new words and phrases every day:

Now when he says his grace after meals he says on his own '…. you good dinner (or tea) 'men'. He continues in the same breath 'Bib off', as he knows that his grace marks the end of the meal.

It was time for the annual trip to Hull Fair:

Joyce, John and the family came to tea, then we all went to the fair. The kiddies thoroughly enjoyed it, and little Michael was really thrilled with everything. I took him on the bumper cars, and he sat on my knee to drive. Then he went on the little roundabout on his own, and later I took him on the Muffin roundabout. Wasn't that the one you took Michael on last year, Darling? In addition, Michael rolled pennies down slots, rolled balls, and I am sure he would have had a go on the shooting range if I had let him. He won you the enclosed cufflinks and a caddy spoon for me. John bought him a policeman's hat and a little bugle, and I bought him a tiny golliwog on elastic. So, as you can see we had a really good time. I wish you could have been with us, Dearest, I miss you so much at times like that.

'A Woman in Love' (no news from Australia)

The days without her husband were dragging, and the evenings were lonely:

Tonight, I have been knitting and listening to our neighbour's TV. It is the Bolshoi Ballet in Swan Lake, at the present. I wish I could see their TV as well as hear it, for I should very much like to see Ulanova, the Russian prima-ballerina.

She continued:

It seems awful to be wishing my life away, but I just cannot help wanting to skip the next few months until we can be together again. Sometimes I feel unbearably lonely. Michael has been a handful lately, too, and I think I shall have to get much firmer with him, or he is going to get out of hand. He is rather too full of his own importance and I do not want him to become 'spoilt'. He can be very obstinate and has a habit of ignoring what he does not want to hear. Your mother says that is a family failing! But, bless him, he really is a darling and I do not know what I should do without him, even though he does almost reduce me to tears at times. I still believe the sooner we have another child, the better it will be for Michael, so I hope by this time next year one is well on the way.

Both Barbara and Michael had developed colds. One of his little playmates had whooping cough, so there was some anxiety lest Michael should catch it. Meanwhile the weather had turned cold, and coal was still rationed:

We are having really wintry weather, snow and hailstones, and bitterly cold winds. I am wondering how our coal will last over the winter, for we have hardly any stock, and as it is so cold, I am using our full allocation now, plus two bags of coke a month.

She continued:

Enough of my moans, and do not pay too much attention to them, dearest, for doubtless we shall pull through, but I would be much happier if I knew you were on your way home.

It seemed increasingly unlikely however that John would be home anytime soon. On 29th October, Israel invaded Egypt. Barbara wrote:

After today's news of the happenings in Egypt, I expect you will remain in Australia, as it is unlikely you will come in this direction now that the Admiralty have stopped ships passing through the Suez Canal. My hopes of you coming ashore are also dwindling, for things seem to be heading towards a general war.

On October 30th, Britain and France sent ultimatums to Israel and Egypt. The following day they started a bombing campaign, while President Nasser of Egypt ordered the sinking of all forty ships currently in the Suez Canal, closing it to shipping thereafter. The bombing campaign targeted Egypt's air force, destroying two hundred of its planes. On October 31st, Barbara wrote:

The Suez situation seems to go from bad to worse. So far, I have not spoken to anyone who approves of the government's action, and the general feeling is that it is rather a 'put-up' job to get the British and French forces in charge of the canal area. Certainly, the rest of the world seems to be against us. Now it sounds as though America is going to support Egypt! I wonder what your views are, Darling.

John would not receive Barbara's letter for nearly three weeks, but on November 3rd he wrote:

The world situation seems to have changed rapidly for the worse during the past few days, and world opinion seems to be that our Government's actions haven't helped matters. That remains to be seen, as well as whether the war will spread. I think the matter should have been left to the United Nations to decide the course of action, but without knowing more about the situation it is difficult to know whether we took the right or wrong action. On the face of it, I would say that it was probably the most unpopular action that Great Britain has taken for some time, but at the same time the countries of the Middle-East only seem to understand force, if the events of the past few years are a guide.

Things were little better on the British Enterprise:

I have been trying to smarten the ship up, but so far with very little success. Sometimes when the work gets on top of me I feel like giving up trying, but eventually things iron out. Meanwhile the overtime goes up, the amount of rust increases, and the stores get used. Goodness knows what will happen when the ship reaches the UK and is inspected again. Anyhow, one has to become resigned to the consequences, otherwise it would worry one sick, and I certainly aren't going to let the ship get me down.

He continued in a lighter vein:

It is now nearly two months since I had my hair cut so I could do with a musical instrument for Christmas. I must try to get ashore in Geraldton for a haircut, although now I have spent all my Australian money – mainly on chocolate which 'Sparks' brings back to sustain me whilst we are working cargo.

They had received orders for Abadan in Iran, and he expected they would return to the UK in February via the Cape of Good Hope, if the Suez crisis had not been resolved. He concluded his letter:

Until I write again, here's sending you all my love and kisses. Kisses which I am saving for my One and Only Love – the dearest, sweetest, kindest, most-loving wife anyone could have. Bye-bye my dearest and may the days roll quickly by to our next reunion, which I hope will be for always.

Although she longed to be with John again, Barbara worried about him returning to the Middle East. On November 3rd, she wrote:

Much as I want you to come home, I would prefer that you were in the much safer area of Australia at the present time. I do hope that your ship is safe and that you do not spend long in the Persian Gulf area, darling. The news is still far from hopeful, isn't it? Anthony Eden is just coming on the radio to make his excuses.

The next day, she continued:

Tonight, Hugh Gaitskell is on the radio whilst I am writing, and he seems to be putting into words what almost everyone is thinking. He finished up by demanding that Eden resigns, as our only hope in the Middle-East situation. I wonder what the result will be.

The Middle-East was not the only worrying world event. On that same day, Russia had invaded Hungary. The Cold War polarisation of the super powers seemed to be worsening:

Listening to the news about Hungary makes me think that Orwell's '1984' may well be a description of the future. It is all very heart-breaking. Where will it all end?

On the 11th November, she added:

The position in Suez does not seem to improve, does it? I wonder whether Russia will carry out her threat to send 'volunteers' to Egypt?

Barbara was also worried that she had not heard from John, although she had learnt from the Journal of Commerce that he was still in Australia:

Still no letter from you, so I am wondering whether you are not well, or over-worked, as you were in port six or seven days ago. I wish you would return to the UK direct from Australia, and then you would be home for Christmas. Do you realise we have only had 108 hours together since December?

The build-up to Christmas in Hull had already started:

Your Mother and Dad were thrilled when we took them to see Father Christmas and the Peter Pan Grotto, as a surprise. Michael thoroughly enjoyed it all and was delighted with the small train he received. My present was a gold-edged tumbler, Mother's was a set of combs, and Dad's was a pair of cufflinks and a tiepin.

Michael had just started going through a shy phase:

It is just possible he may be a bit shy with you at first, when next we see you, Darling, so do not worry if he won't have anything to do with you at first. Of course, he may not be, as he is always chattering about 'my Daddy' and 'my Daddy's ship' and recognises every photograph of you.

Blue Moon (Australia to India)

Barbara finally received John's letter from Geraldton, Australia, on November 14th, after a wait of nearly three weeks without news. It was clear that he would not be home for Christmas after all. She hoped it would be the last one they would ever spend apart. At least he would be back for her birthday in February, when the ship dry-docked, and this time he would be home for good. Meanwhile he had received another change of orders and was heading for Bombay. They would load a cargo there and take it a few hundred miles north to the port of Kandla in the Gulf of Kutch, also in India. The blockage of the Suez Canal had caused many tankers to be re-routed. He guessed that the journey home from India would need to be via the Cape of Good Hope. Of course, when he got home, the condition of the ship would be inspected. John was still struggling to keep on top of the rust and his relations with the Captain were still somewhat strained:

I seem to be getting along moderately with the Old Man, although we have rumpuses every now and again. I am quite sure his report about me at the end of the trip will be far from favourable, but as I am leaving the company then it won't matter a lot.

Meanwhile Barbara had heard some news that put John's return to the UK in doubt:

Do you know if there is any truth in the rumour I heard yesterday that ships at the other side of the Cape would not return to the UK for dry-docking, but would go instead to Australian dock-yards? More important, is this likely to happen to you, darling? A report in today's Journal of Commerce, that only the bigger tankers would be used to bring oil round the Cape, seems to back up the rumour. Dearest one, I do hope that you return to the UK soon, for I have never wanted you more. This long separation is only bearable by the thought that we shall be together again in February, but if you dry-dock in Australia you may be away another year. I am now even more anxious to hear your next orders, sweetheart.

On December 8th she wrote:

Last night I dreamed that you were in dry-dock and I was with you. Your ship seemed to have shrunk in size externally, yet your cabin was just the same. In my dream you were very tired – too tired to even kiss me, so I am wondering whether you are in fact feeling the strain. Do let me know, sweetheart, just how you are, and whether you are not too well. It was a very clear dream, but I do hope that you are quite fit, darling. I shall be wondering now until I get your next letter. Aren't I silly?

They had now been separated for a full year, apart from the short visits Barbara had made to the ship at Finnart and Liverpool. Michael had only seen his father once in that time, although John would send little letters and drawings to him. Barbara wrote:

Michael's latest is to put any toy which needs repairing back into the cupboard, with the words 'Daddy mend it'.

'My Prayer' (India to Aden)

On December 16th, John received orders to proceed from Calcutta to Little Aden:

Of course, it could mean any port around the Persian Gulf, but we are all hoping the cargo will be for Land's End for Orders.

Back home, Barbara was busy preparing the house for Christmas, once Michael had gone to bed:

I gave the sitting room a thorough clean, washed the floors etc and rearranged the furniture. Then I put up the decorations and the Christmas Tree. At nearly 10pm I was digging in the garden to fill the bucket with soil, and it was almost midnight by I got to bed. This morning I switched the fairy lights on before Michael came downstairs, and his little face was a picture when he looked around. If only you could have seen him, darling. He said 'Oh pwitties, Michael's pwitties, Michael's twee'.

On 22nd December, Barbara received a telegram from John. She responded:

I hope the fact that you are going to South West Africa means you are working your way back to the UK.

She had been sewing nighties for her nieces as Christmas presents:

I finished them off tonight whilst listening to a Dickens play on the radio. All his stories are on the morbid side, aren't they? But they are supposed to be true of life at that time, and looking at modern times, similar things happen. For instance, the uprising in Hungary makes me think of 'A Tale of Two Cities'.

She tried to smarten Michael up for Christmas:

He must have his hair cut as it is sticking out at all angles again. Why do you both have such shocking hair? At least with a girl it could be grown long and plaited, but I hope if we ever have a daughter she will inherit her mother's hair!

Barbara kept having to replace bulbs on the fairy lights:

Michael insists they are on all his waking hours, so I hope they are not too heavy on the electric. He likes plenty of light, and as soon as the daylight fades, he says 'Dark now, light on'. You like plenty of light too, don't you darling, so he must take after you. I think he is more like you than me really, so he will make a good husband for some fortunate girl, but I guess he will have a good time first (also like his Daddy??). Doesn't it make you feel old when you think of Michael getting married?

On Christmas Eve, she took Michael to the Children's Carol Service:

Michael loved it but kept up a running commentary on everything he saw. 'Baby Jesus there – moo-cow, Mummy – pretty tree – lights – where Jesus gone etc.'

She then spent Christmas day with her parents, her brothers, their wives and her three nieces. Her sister-in-law was expecting again, and they were hoping this time for a boy. Meanwhile her brother showered Michael with gifts of cars and trains. Barbara listed all the presents they had given and received:

We have had a very happy day, but I wish you could have been with us, Dearest.

A few days later it was Barbara and John's third wedding anniversary. John sent a bouquet of chrysanthemums and daffodils, much to Barbara's delight:

I had been feeling rather despondent about spending yet another anniversary without you, but your beautiful flowers cheered me up immensely.

Both sets of parents came to tea:

We had a little anniversary party, without the most important person, but we drank your health and you were constantly in my thoughts.

On New Year's Eve, Barbara wrote:

I have just been thinking of New Year's Eve three years ago, and the fun we had in celebrating it. I can remember everything we did. I wonder whether I shall always be able to. Can you remember our honeymoon in detail, darling? Although a lot seems to have happened since then, it does not really seem three years. I think the past year has been the longest, so let us hope the New Year will bring us more time together. It could hardly bring us less!

'Make it a Party' (Aden to South Africa)

With Christmas over, she was busy baking in preparation for celebrating Michael's second birthday:

Tonight, I have iced the birthday cake. It is a rainbow sponge, and I have iced it in pink, edged with chocolate. In alphabet cachous I have put HAPPY BIRTHDAY MICHAEL, and above it in silver balls I have made a figure 2, and at the bottom of the letters are the two candles. It looks quite nice, even though I say it myself!

The party seemed to have been a success:

Entertaining little ones like that is quite easy. They can only play Ring-a-Roses, so for the rest I just let them play with all Michael's toys, and they sorted themselves out quite well. I also had a good supply of balloons, which are always very popular. I think your Dad was amazed at the noise, but it was the first young children's party he had been to, so he had not known what to expect.

John sent Michael a birthday telegram:

The telegraph boy woke us up at 7 am, and Michael opened the envelope himself. He was particularly pleased with it because there were soldiers on the telegram.

There was also a Ship Letter Telegram for Barbara, which read:

SORRY NO LETTER POSTED ADEN SPECULATE SEVENTY DAYS MORE HOME ALL WELL MY LOVE ALWAYS = JOHN.

Barbara was hoping he might be home a little earlier than seventy days. She was wondering which UK port he would be dry-docking in and whether he had applied for his leave yet. After that, he would be home for good. He would be on his way now from Aden to South Africa:

Have you managed to catch up on lost sleep during your trip down from Aden? I do hope that you are building yourself up for coming home, also that you arrive in the UK mid-February, although I shall be very happy to see you, sweetheart, whenever you come, for I want you in more ways than one.

She had given the veranda a facelift by cleaning it and hanging new curtains:

Whilst I was cleaning the light fitment, it came off in my hand. After it had dried again, I screwed it back on, but it does not work, and it is not only the bulb which has fused. So like Michael, I am saying 'Daddy mend it'. I can probably manage a few weeks, providing I do not decide to wash at night.

Barbara had decided however that some of Michael's toys could not wait a few more weeks to be mended, so she tackled the job herself while Michael was in bed:

Well, this morning whilst I was washing up Michael came flying through and, showing me part of his train, said 'Look Mummy, Daddy mend it for Michael!' He must think you paid us a flying visit overnight, Darling. I wish that it were possible.

It had again been weeks since Barbara received a letter from John, but she kept up her daily instalment, detailing every hour of how she spent her days:

I wonder how many pages I have written since you were last home. I expect my letters read rather like Mrs Dale's Diary. Although I enjoy writing to you Darling, I am looking forward to the time when I have no need to. I do hope that I shall be getting a telegram to say you are on your way home.

The radio was still her main source of news:

On the whole I think the world opinion is that Eden's retirement is a good move. I wonder how Mr McMillan will make out, and whether there will be an election soon.

151

On January 21st, she wrote:

I wonder whether you have now rounded the Cape and are northward bound. I am longing for you so much, my Dearest, that the next few weeks cannot pass quickly enough.

'Knee Deep in the Blues' (South Africa to Nigeria)

When the much-awaited telegram arrived the next day, it brought bad news. The British Enterprise would not after all be returning to the UK for repairs but would remain in South Africa. Whatever her first reaction may have been, Barbara put on a brave face:

It was a great disappointment to learn that you are going back to Durban to dry-dock. I had felt so sure that in three or four weeks we would be together. Still, I suppose we must just 'grin and bear it' and hope that you soon will be bound for the UK. It looks as though you will still be at sea when your contract ends. If you do not re-sign, will they bring you back to the UK more quickly?

John's next letter included more information:

By now you will know our orders regarding dry-docking in Durban. This trip seems to have lasted an eternity, but I am convinced that once the canal is open for navigation again, it won't be long before we go through it in the right direction. What I am afraid of is being landed on the Aden-Greece run again, but even so I think we should get orders for the UK as soon as conditions revert back to normal. Hence it looks as if I shall have a summer leave after all – only one summer late.

Writing a letter was also an opportunity for John to vent his frustration:

I expect you will have realised that I am still hand over head with work. We are two sailors short of the full crew, leaving only the Boatswain and two sailors from the watch to do all the work. This, plus the fact that there are no apprentices, means that I can get very little work done without payment of overtime, which also adds to my work. Up to now I have filled up 18 double sided overtime sheets in duplicate – each an hour or so's work.

I think I mentioned a while back that there is rust everywhere and it is a constant battle to keep it within bounds. Well, the Captain has just realised that something is bound to be said if the ship reaches home in this condition and true to his nature he is making sure that he gets none of the blame. Every other day I have to hear lectures from him on how he used to run ships as Mate and the praise he got when they reached home. Some blame he puts on the Boatswain who is not very cooperative and is not very efficient at organising the crew. However, I get most of the blame for not bringing the Boatswain to heel more, and for not organising the work properly.

I have seen the confidential report the Old Man was going to send in about me, had we gone to the UK and it was certainly not good. The Old Man urges me to pick on the Boatswain and pull him up for every little fault until I find a big enough fault to get him logged for, but it is not in my nature to continually find fault in a person or to try to pass the blame onto somebody else all the time.

Anyway, I listen to all the Old Man's lectures and I tell the Boatswain off about any major faults and those minor ones I consider necessary. I try to carry out the running of the ship to the best of my ability, at the same time as tending to the Old Man's whims. However, the way I look at it, it is no good getting upset about it. A bad report won't do me a lot of harm if I am leaving the company anyway – all the same, I should have liked a better one. The last Mate on this ship must have worried too much about it – hence why he was paid off.

The Captain says I have very little system, which has perhaps some truth in it, but I have hardly had time to sit down and think up systems. Sometimes I manage to find time to do a proper dhobi, but very often I have to rub out a shirt and a pair of shorts just before I need them. I would have an easier time if I accepted a lower standard for the ship and its equipment, but I always aim higher than I think I can accomplish. The only trouble is that the Old Man has an even higher standard.

Before dry-docking in Durban, the British Enterprise would discharge part of the cargo at Ango Ango in the Belgian Congo and the rest at Lagos in Nigeria. This would give John an opportunity to send and receive letters, as he had not sent or received any since before Christmas. When Barbara finally received his letter, she was forthright in her opinions of the Captain:

Poor Darling, you certainly do have a lot to put up with from the Captain. I do not know how you refrain from telling him a few home truths. I am afraid I should be doing so. As I think you realised, I was not impressed by what I saw of him, and I have met his type at work. It is a safe bet to assume that when he was Mate he pushed as much work as possible onto the Second Mate – along with lectures on what he had to do when Second – and spent as much time as possible toadying to the Captain. Honestly, his type makes me sick. So far as giving you a bad report, I do not think it will stand to much account with the Company, for you have always had excellent reports in the past, and by now they will have realised this Captain never praises anyone. Anyway sweetheart, I know which is the better and more intelligent one, and I would have none other than you for my beloved. By the way, his wife told me that her husband hoped to have a long trip, as he did not want his leave until the summer, so he will be pleased about the change of orders. I pity that poor woman!

One evening Barbara was baby-sitting for her sister-in-law:

I am watching 'Animal, Vegetable and Mineral' on TV, and it is quite interesting. Also, it takes my mind off the previous programme, which was a very true-to-life film about the Merchant Navy in wartime. Rather too vivid for my liking, although it had its lighter moments.

Michael was very keen on watching TV, whenever he got the opportunity, and was quick to re-enact what he saw:

Have you seen or heard Elvis Presley? Michael can copy his actions perfectly and 'rocks' like an expert. I shall have to censure what he listens to, as he picks up lots of expressions from the radio. After listening to 'Educating Archie', he told me to 'get going'. We are now entering the time when we must remember that 'little pitchers have big ears'.

'The Girl Can't Help It' (Nigeria and Belgian Congo)

She had told John's parents about John's deferred return to the UK:

Of course, they were disappointed that you will not be home as soon as we hoped, but your mother said it will be nicer that you are home in the warmer weather. (I wish I could think that way – I would not mind you shivering with us!) Whilst I was knitting this evening, I have been indulging in a wonderful daydream. It was that, by some means or other, I could fly out to Durban, to be with you whilst the ship dry-docks. I know it sounds crazy, but I have worked out all the details concerning Michael, clothes etc. All I need is a fairy godmother to wave her wand! Oh well, there's no harm in wishing. I imagine there are quite a lot of disgruntled men on board, having started to come up this way and then turning back. I suppose there is a reason, but I am sure it is not necessary.

She continued:

I do not think I have yet got over the shock of hearing you will not be coming back in the next few weeks. I was so sure that you were coming. It does not help matters when friendly shopkeepers and neighbours ask, 'Any news of your husband coming home?' I think they believe you have deserted me!

Not only did Barbara have to deal with the disappointment of John's delayed return, but she was also worrying about her brother, also called John, who was at sea nearer home, on the Kingston Amber trawler:

It seems that whenever John is nearing home, we have very bad weather with high winds and heavy rain, or so it has been lately. John is expected home on Wednesday and I should imagine he will be glad to be ashore for the 60-odd hours, as many older trawlermen say this weather is the worst for many years. I woke about four-thirty this morning and the wind and rain were so fierce I could not get to sleep again for wondering about John. He is only on a small trawler, and two or three trawlers have been lost on the coast.

In January 1955, the Hull trawlers Lorella and Roderigo were lost with all hands when they were caught in a Force Ten gale. They had battled against the weather for days and were then overwhelmed by black ice, causing the trawlers to capsize. The last radio message transmitted by the Roderigo had been 'Listing to starboard and going over; cannot abandon ship'. Yet these were more modern ships than the Amber, which was built in 1937 and had been requisitioned during the war. To Barbara's relief her brother returned safely on this occasion and did not return to sea immediately after his 60 hours ashore:

John's ship has had to go in for repair, so he is at home again. He is trying to get another ship if he can, as the Amber is not the last word in comfort. Also, they are constantly having to go to ports for minor repairs, which reduces their catch.

Her brother and sister-in-law were also awaiting the imminent arrival of their fourth child, but before long he was back at sea, again on the Kingston Amber. Before he left, he helped Barbara choose an electric washing machine, although he would have to wait for a more successful trip before he could buy one for his own growing family. Knowing that he would not be heading home as planned, John had sent money for Barbara to buy herself a washing machine for her birthday. She seems to have appreciated the gift:

It is sweet of you to send me money to buy an electric washer, dearest, and it certainly will be a wonderful present, as I do think they are very useful (especially when our family increases), and they save a lot of hard work and time. If I am to have a washer, shall I advertise the wringer for sale?

Now she knew that John would not be back anytime soon, Barbara threw herself into home-improvement, leaving Michael with John's parents while she started redecorating the little dining room. She was again concerned that her in-laws were struggling financially:

Your Dad is having to have his trousers washed regularly, and he has got down to only his best suit trousers, as he put his knee through his flannels the other day. Your mother said she would like to get him some more strong flannels, but at present did not see how she could manage it. I did suggest she took the money out of your Beverley account, but she said she would see if she could manage without doing so. I wonder if you think it a good idea to buy your Dad some flannels as an advance birthday present, as I know he really does need them.

Your Dad has at last decided to sell his printing machine. I think it is probably as well, for every time he goes into the office he gets a bad cold. It also affects his 'waterworks'. The doctor says it is only his age and nothing to worry about. It does mean your mother has a washday every day though. Apart from that, he is well and making good progress with the rug he is making for us. You know, Darling, I think I really am as interested in the well-being of your parents as of mine, and I do try to do what you would do if you were at home. But I do realise that you will have to have a discussion with your mother when you come home, as daughters-in-law can't always say the same as sons!

In addition to the £80 to buy a washing machine, John sent flowers for Barbara's birthday in February. She responded:

I am really thrilled with the flowers as they bring such a promise of spring. Tulips, daffodils, double-headed narcissi, irises, anemones, and some small red flowers that look and smell like roses. My Dad says he thinks they belong to the peony family. Thank you, sweetheart, for the loving thought. Michael gave me a little bunch of anemones too. In fact, he gave me them about half a dozen times and each time sang 'Happy Birthday to Mummy'. I have now fourteen birthday cards, so for an old woman of 28 I have done very well.

'Baby, Baby'

It was now exactly a year since Barbara's brief visit to the ship at Finnart and fourteen months that John had been away from home. When her sister-in-law, Joyce, had another baby girl, Michael was fascinated:

He is really interested in the baby and keeps saying 'Mummy get a baby'. I tell him we shall have to wait until Daddy comes home. I hope by then he has forgotten, or he will expect you to produce one immediately.

Michael was also starting to ask a lot of questions:

Michael hates the bath plug to be pulled out before he gets all his toys out, and lately he has worried about where the water goes. So I told him that it went through the pipes, into the drains, and then into the sea for Daddy's ship to sail on. Now that he has an explanation, he seems much happier.

The two-year-old was now three feet tall and weighed over two and a half stones:

Have you ever been to the Custom Office 'collecting room' in Hull? I went today to pay duty on, and collect, 100 cigarettes for my brother. We had to go through a passageway in Scale Lane, through a back door, then up several flights of stairs. I expected arriving on the roof any minute, but eventually we arrived at the right room and the clerk asked me to sit down – was I glad! I had carried Michael most of the way, and he is no lightweight.

'Look Homeward, Angel' (Back to Durban)

Whilst in Hull old town, Barbara went to pay John's £5 fee to the Navigators and Engineering Officers' Union at Friary Chambers in Whitefriargate. She had another chat with Mr Upton:

He said if you were 'willing to break your heart for £125 per month', he could possibly get you twelve months as Master with the Holderness Steam Coasting Company. It would be coasting round the UK and very hard work, but at least it would give you the required period in command which is needed for many shore jobs. In any case, he said he hopes you will see him when you come home on leave.

At Ango Ango, John finally received Barbara's letters describing how they had spent Christmas and Michael's birthday, together with the photograph she had sent him as a Christmas present. It was taken by a professional photographer but in their own home, so that John could see the new wallpaper in the living room, as well as his wife and son. John replied:

It was the best Christmas present I could have had in the circumstances. Next Christmas, however, I should like to be at home with you as my present.

Work on board the British Enterprise was still relentless, although there were some improvements:

Now that the ship is not going home for a while, we have stopped painting her. The Boatswain paid off into hospital at Ango Ango so we have promoted an A.B. to Boatswain and I feel much happier with him than the last one.

Barbara, meanwhile, was thinking that their house needed a facelift:

It will soon be time to have the exterior of the house painted. What colour do you think, darling, now that next door have had theirs painted cherry? I wondered about turquoise and cream, which is quite popular now, and also a good wearing colour, or there is a very nice creamy brown which is fashionable.

Again, she was waiting for news:

I waited in vain for the postman this morning. I wonder whether there is a letter from you on its way yet. It seems ages since I last heard from you, but I keep hoping, and quite understand that you have been very busy. I hope you will have opportunity to relax and enjoy yourself in Durban. After all, on the other ships you have been on, the Second Mate had to work harder than Mate, so why not on the Enterprise? Don't tell me – I know!! Still, do try to get some pleasure, Sweetheart.

On February 17th, John wrote from Durban:

The Old Man sent a confidential report in about me and it certainly wasn't a very good one. However, one can but do one's best. Today the Old Man received my renewal contract, but I have declined to sign it, so from the first week next month I shall be off contract. However, until we return to the UK my present rate of wages and leave will still stand. The reason I gave to the Old Man for not signing was that I did not wish to be bound at the present time. I doubt whether this will have any effect on the proximity of my next return to the UK, but several British Tanker crews have been released after serving about a year away and I shall soon have completed 15 months. Of course, the sailors and firemen have only done about 7 months on board so far. Although we are now three sailors short, I doubt whether we shall be taking any more in Durban as jailbirds and deserters are about all we can pick up.

I could have kicked myself in Lagos for I had £3 stolen from my room. Of course, I had been careless and had left my door open for a few moments. I also gave a local some of my clothes to launder. Later I regretted it, as I thought he had made off with them. However, he brought them back an hour or so before we sailed, and they had certainly had some rough treatment – they were tattered and torn and, although stiff with starch, they were not particularly clean. Now I am urgently needing white shirts, shoes and underpants, but so far, I have not had the opportunity of getting ashore during the day.

Yesterday evening I went ashore with a number of the other Officers. We listened to some very good 'Rock and Roll' music on an organ and drums, and then went to see the film 'Anastasia', which I found very entertaining. It is the first film I have seen since I was home last. Later we went to the Merchant Navy Officers' Club, where a dance was in progress. I didn't do any dancing however for I don't really enjoy dancing with anyone but you, and at such a time I feel poignantly lonely and full of longing for you. On board the ship, work occupies practically all my time and I have not time to think deeply of other things. However, ashore I see other men with their wives and sweethearts and I wish that I were with you. Some men of course find substitutes, but for me I could never transfer any of the affection I feel for you to anyone else. To me we are as one, and when we are separated there is a blank emptiness that you and you alone can fill. We shall just have to hope and pray that we shall soon be united again.

'Around the World' (Durban to India via Iran)

Barbara had developed a nervous rash, which her doctor put down to her disappointment over John's non-return. He prescribed her some tablets which made her sleepy, so she was struggling to concentrate on her sewing and knitting during the evenings. She found that she made particularly slow progress with knitting:

> *This is urgent. What colour pullover would you like in 3½ years' time? This is a serious question, Darling. Do you like fawn, or yellow, or brown?*

John replied:

> *Perhaps you had better wait until I come home before you choose the wool for my pullover. I think I should prefer maroon to yellow.*

As usual, she listened to the radio while she sewed and knitted:

> *The 10 pm news has just come on and I hear the Canal could be open in ten days, so let's keep hoping!*

The British Enterprise was on its way from Durban to Abadan in Iran to load cargo. However, they would be taking it to Karachi in Pakistan, rather than heading towards Suez. John sent Barbara a telegram on March 7th to let her know. Barbara was philosophical about it:

> *Never mind, our luck is bound to change soon, and I often remind myself that I have so much to be thankful for, most of all for the knowledge that no matter what distance divides us, our love for each other is unchanged. Even so, I am longing for the day when I can show my love for you more actively. I am fully recovered now, with a much more balanced outlook, and have even put on an odd pound or two. I shall be a real fatty by the time you come home, darling!*

A couple of days later, she added:

> *I heard on the 9 pm news that an earthquake and great tidal wave had affected the North Pacific, so I got out the atlas to see if you were in that area. I do hope you were not affected, darling. Whilst studying the map, I discovered that West India is not so far from Abadan after all. Don't laugh but I thought India was much further south, almost parallel with Africa. You certainly have an ignorant wife!*

John again encountered problems, loading cargo in Abadan:

Once again, the cargo didn't go quite as planned. The first two grades were loaded to a fraction of a ton of the ordered quantity. Then I left the Third Mate to watch the next parcel, and to let me know when there was about 100 tons to go. The next thing I heard, he came up and told me he had loaded 33 tons too much. After we had finished loading, the Old Man asked me to have a few drinks with him and the pilot. Personally, all I wanted to do was to turn in, as I get little sleep loading cargo. Anyhow the Old Man told the Second and Third Mates they would have to do an extra hour each on watch, so I didn't have to go on watch until 6 am. However, I was still not prepared for the session to last until 3 in the morning.

He was anxious to replenish his wardrobe:

When we received orders for Bombay, I had visions of buying some more gear, but I believe Karachi is not so good for that. I am really at rock bottom. Of the only two pairs of shoes I possess, one has a sole which is split across the centre and the other has a sole which flaps open as I walk, so I shall have to do some cobbling. I am down to two pairs of underpants and although better off for vests, most of them are torn. Tropical shirts I can boast of three, but all are torn to a greater or lesser degree and are really ready for dumping. Other tropical gear is on a par with this, so if I don't get some soon I shall be like a ragman.

The ship, too, was looking worse for wear:

The rust is peeling off the ship in great patches and I still have a lot of the repaired work to cover up, so I don't know how I can possibly get her looking smart. However, the main thing is to get the orders for home, and I shall just have to smarten up the ship the best I can. Several of the Engineers wrote from Abadan to enquire of the possibility of us being relieved abroad, so we are hopefully awaiting the answer. Apparently, some British tanker crews have been flown home from the Middle East, so you never know when I may be dropping in. I am just waiting for the time when I can hold you once more in my arms and shower you with all the kisses I am saving up for you. It seems like an eternity since I last had you in my arms, and it is getting on for sixteen months since I was home.

Barbara was also missing John:

I seem to have a fit of the blues tonight, and my good resolutions seem to have fled, so I must try and write the blues away. It seems an age since I last heard from you, darling, and I am missing you terribly. I had a secret hope that you might fly home from Abadan, but obviously you are not doing so. Michael has returned to his favourite question: 'When Daddy coming home?' I suppose it is because I had said so assuredly that you would be home soon. Tonight, Michael said, 'Michael go on puff-puff to see Daddy on ship and bring him home'. I wish it were as easy as that!

She was finding that Michael could communicate his needs more clearly now:

I was just going to start writing when Michael called down. When I went upstairs, he said 'Dat one not there'. His little arm was quite cold, so I presume he had left it out of the covers and it was numb, so I rubbed it until he said brightly 'Come back now'. Then he snuggled down and went to sleep.

On March 23rd she received the letter which John had posted from Karachi. She replied:

I hope you bought yourself some more clothes at Karachi. You really have let yourself get very low What have you done about your shoes? I cannot imagine 'Dear Ronnie' being very pleased about his Chief Officer walking in shoes which flap! I am more than ever convinced that you need me to keep an eye on you, darling.

John wrote in a later letter:

I managed to buy three white shirts in Calcutta, so they will last me a while. I also bought a pair of khaki shorts – supposedly made to measure – but now I find they are much too big around the waist. They will do me when I have been home a few months and put on some weight.

Barbara would have agreed that John needed to put on weight. His letter from Calcutta contained a photograph of him taken at Christmas. Barbara commented:

You look to be very brown, but also very thin, Darling, though you are giving me a lovely smile. Michael was thrilled with the new picture of Daddy, and we both had to kiss you several times.

'When I Fall in Love' (India to Iran)

A couple of days later there was a surprise parcel from John, with instructions not to open it until March 27th, the anniversary of their first meeting. She took it up to bed with her so that she could open it with Michael first thing in the morning:

> *It is a lovely casket of chocolates and looks so nice it is a shame to open it, but I shall be able to use the casket when the chocolates have gone. Michael was thrilled with his sweets and ate the two lollipops before we got up. There was also a roll of chocolate drops, a bus of mint creams, a box of chocolate cigarettes, and a Robin Hood whose tummy and legs are all bags of different sweets.*

She continued:

> *I am so glad that you came to the Mission four years ago today, for the past four years have been the happiest years of my life. Even though we have been parted so much, at least I can feel secure in your precious love. I am sure we shall always be as happy if we continue to love each other, and you can be sure that my love for you, dearest, will never weaken but grow even more during the years, if that is possible, for I love you with all my being. I wonder if we shall be four by next year.*

Since her miscarriage in the autumn of 1955, Barbara had been suffering from intermittent bleeding. At the end of March 1957, she was finally taken into the Hull Hospital for Women to have an operation, while Michael stayed at her mother's:

> *Well it is all over and done with, and I am making a rapid recovery. Apart from a slightly swimmy head, I feel fine, and the nurse has just told me I look a fraud lying in bed with rosy cheeks. It is a lovely hospital in beautiful grounds. There are only four beds in each part of the ward and the massive windows open out onto the lawn. The nursing staff are very friendly and very informal, even the Matron, who has a word with everyone each day.*

> *Yesterday was truly a lost day. We were given a cup of tea at 5.30 am, then about 9.30 were given an injection, then put on the stretcher trolley. That is all I remember. I went off without the anaesthetic, although I expect I was given one. The next thing I knew it was 3.20 pm and I dozed the rest of the day. I was very amused to learn that the first thing I said when I was coming*

round after the anaesthetic was 'I don't want anything, thank you.' I have no recollection of saying it, but the nurse assured me I said it very sweetly. We were given a slice of toast and a cup of tea about six, as we were good girls and had not been sick.

Since the surgeons made their rounds this afternoon, there has been lots of merriment. One of the nurses got into bed with one of the patients and started moaning about every pain imaginable. Then she rang the bell for the Sister, but before she came she hid under the bed and grabbed the Sister's legs as she went by.

The food here is excellent and more than enough for me. In fact, I do not think there is a nicer hospital. I think I shall try to get into this nursing home when our next baby is on the way. I wish you could pay me a visit tonight, sweetheart. I miss you more than ever when the other husbands arrive. I wonder whether you will be home by May.

Barbara spent a couple of days at her mother's to recuperate when she came out of hospital:

I must admit I have thoroughly enjoyed my stay in hospital. I have not laughed so much for a long time! The nurses were full of fun, and there was no formality at all. Before I left this morning, I was asked if I wanted to make an advance booking for the maternity section!

John, meanwhile, was continuing to have misfortunes on board ship:

On our way up to Calcutta, we had to anchor overnight part of the way up the river. I was just congratulating myself on having the cargo intact when the ship's watchman rang me up from aft to say that all the ropes we use for making fast aft had been stolen. When I went aft, I found four heavy mooring ropes and a towing line had gone. Thieves had come aboard and paid them out over the stern and then towed them away. I knew ropes had been stolen at that place before and I had two men watching the ropes, but one of them left the poop for about eighteen minutes and the deed was done. It will cost the company the best part of £1000 to replace them so I hope they don't stop my Eastern Bonus as a contribution.

Barbara's brother's trawler had also had a costly trip:

It was reported in the paper that his trawler had been taken in by the Russians, for going over the boundary. When he eventually got home, he said they were only 2 degrees inside the Russian boundary line, but they were fined £1000 and their gear was confiscated. It will cost approximately £5000 altogether and the skipper has been suspended. There have been a number of incidents between trawlers and the Russians during the last few days.

Now the father of four little girls, her brother had bought his nephew a gun and holster:

Michael was thrilled with it and he spent the rest of the afternoon 'shooting' us, as his favourite game is Cowboys and Indians.

John's next telegram put paid to her hopes that he would be back in May. Barbara responded:

Although I did not really expect that you would be coming home, I still felt very disappointed when I learnt from your telegram that you are going to Burma from Abadan. I am longing to be with you, my dearest. It is such an age since we were together and then it was for an all too brief period. It will be almost like being newly-wed when you do come home, sweetheart! I feel if I do not hear some better news from you soon, I shall do something desperate – like setting out to meet you in some distant land! I do hope the Government decide to use that wretched Canal before you arrive at Abadan.

'Putting on the Style' (Iran to Burma)

She had bought herself a new outfit for Easter:

I have had a little spending spree and bought myself a new suit in a sort of blue-green, a pair of red shoes and red handbag, and a new white blouse. To complete the outfit, I bought a green straw hat, trimmed with velvet. I shall wear it on Easter Sunday if it is warm enough, then it will be put away until you come home. I hope you will like it, dearest, for I bought it specially for your home-coming. It may surprise you how much I plan my life and work for 'when John comes home'. That seems to be the phrase that crops up most of all in my conversation and thoughts, and now Michael does the same. You would be amazed at what he is going to do 'when Daddy comes home'. I think that the most important thing is that Daddy is bringing baby Alison! It has got to be a baby girl for Michael. I am trying to discourage this talk about babies, otherwise he will be very disappointed when he finds that Daddy has not got a baby in his case after all. I hope that you spend a Happy Easter, dearest, and that you do not have to work too hard.

On April 27th, she wrote:

I was rudely awoken from sleep this morning by the telegraph boy banging on the door. However, I was delighted that he did when I opened your telegram and learned that at last something definite has been decided. I guess that you will be relieved when your ship returns to Abadan from Burma, but I am wondering whether you will be coming by sea or air. When I told Michael your news, he bounced on the bed shouting 'Daddy coming home! Daddy coming home!'

John's next letter explained:

When we were in Abadan the Old Man received a letter from the Company saying they were considering relieving all those who wanted relief at an early opportunity. Of course, I was one of the first to put my name down and everyone else followed suit, including the Old Man.

Things have gone fairly smoothly on board and the loading of the cargo in Abadan went quite well this time. I slipped up however in not taking much fresh water, much to the Chief Engineer's disgust as it meant he had to use fuel to distil salt water for use in the boilers.

The last couple of days I have been giving my room a big clear out and incidentally sorting what gear I shall need to carry in the plane and what will have to come by sea. There is quite a pile of things to dump. I think I shall dump my old uniform jacket, battledress jacket and blue raincoat as they are all very shabby. Some things though I am retaining for gardening, although they are useless for much else.

It is now 17 months since I went down to Falmouth to join the Talent and it seems to have been 17 years, the way I have missed you.

Barbara meanwhile was getting the house ready for John's return. The outside of the house had been repainted, the front gate had been replaced, and she had bought material for new net curtains. She also had good news:

Did you know that after five years of buying a house, you can claim an income tax rebate for all repairs and decorations done in that time?

There was further news on the Suez Canal:

It has just been announced that any member countries of the Canal Users' Association are free to use the Canal 'under protest'. I wonder what our government will decide. I worked out tonight that you could be home in about 5½ weeks if you come through the Canal, but of course if you fly from Abadan it will be even sooner.

'Too Much' (Back to India)

On May 24th, however, Barbara wrote:

What an anti-climax it was to receive your telegram last night. I felt so sure you would be coming home, and I have spent all week cleaning the house and putting up fresh curtains so that everything would be nice for your return. You will be disappointed too, darling, for I gathered from your letter that you really thought you would be flying home. July seems an awful long way away and it feels as if you never will be home, sweetheart. I cannot see why it is going to take you so long either. Surely it does not take a month from Abadan, or are your engines slowing down?

I am afraid you will have a week's gap in my letters, as I have not written this week, as I expected you would be home before they reached you. I do hope you understand, dearest, and do not think I have forgotten you. That I shall never do, no matter how long we are parted.

John explained:

We are on our way home, but it is by a devious route. Tomorrow we should arrive at Bombay where we are loading a cargo to take to Cochin and Kandla, both ports on the west coast of India. Then we shall go to Abadan to load a cargo for Land's End for Orders, via the Suez Canal. Hence the proposed relieving by air is off, and we shall be relieved when we deliver the cargo at its destination. Coming home on the ship means we shall have store manifest, half yearly indents and such-like to complete, so I shall be kept busy for the next six weeks. The ship is going to look in a terrible state when we reach home, but I can't do any painting just now as during the monsoon it rains nearly every day. Also, the crew have already had nearly 1,000 hours overtime and they do not want any more. Many are the dodges they try to work either to miss overtime or to get paid for overtime without working. At the present, two of the crew reckon they are too sick to work overtime, and another is bedridden. Still another has his right hand in a plaster cast for six weeks, and the remainder dodge when they can. The crux of it is that the whole of the crew are absolutely fed up. Most of them were banking on being flown home from Bombay so they also feel let down.

Whilst we were at Budge Budge, I had my first trip ashore since leaving Durban. However, it was not for pleasure, for the police had recaptured some of our stolen ropes and I had to go along to identify them. It was a really hot day and I had to travel about 20 miles to the police station to see the ropes and then return the same distance by car, so it was a warm outing. Nevertheless, I did see a good part of the Indian countryside and it was a most interesting run around.

I was working out that if we pay off about the 15th July I shall have about 4 months leave due to me, having completed over 19 months on the Talent and this ship. Fancy thinking I should be taking my leave after 6 months when I was on the Talent. It will have certainly been the longest year of our married life – since we were in Dingle. The trip on the Talent alone seemed to be an eternity, and every day I miss you more and more. I expect Michael bears little resemblance to the little boy who was on the ship at Dingle and still less to the baby just learning to walk, when I was home last. It seems almost a dream to think we shall be together in another six weeks, and I am longing to hold you in my arms at last. You can tie a chain around my neck then to make sure I don't go away again.

When Barbara found out from the Journal of Commerce that the British Enterprise was going to Kandla from Bombay, she wrote:

No wonder it is taking you so long to come home. You know, I still feel annoyed with the Company for not flying you home. It seems so wrong that you should be away all this long time.

'Don't Forbid Me' (India via Abadan to Land's End for Orders)

She was planning the seaside holiday they could have together in August:

Surely you will be home by August, dearest. I am seriously thinking of asking Dr Donaldson to write to the Company asking for your relief on compassionate grounds, if you do not get home by July. He told me that lack of normal married life is having an adverse effect on my health, so I am sure he would oblige if necessary.

John must have been reading her mind, for he wrote:

I don't think the company would dare to send us elsewhere after Abadan or they would just be risking wholesale desertions. Even if the Canal closed, I think they would send us home by air without hesitation.

In Barbara's next letter, a telephone number appears in the top left-hand corner. She writes:

I wonder what your reaction is to the addition to our address. I hope you are not annoyed about it, but in case you are, let me tell you how it came about. For some time now, I have thought that for us to have a telephone would make it much better for our parents, particularly yours, to contact us quickly, as it is quite inconvenient to accept calls at our neighbours. I also thought that in the event of you getting a shore job, or one where you are coasting, and possibly wanting to contact me quickly, a phone of our own would be a great advantage. I hope you will agree that it is not an unnecessary expense, when I tell you it will cost £8-10-0 a year, which is 3/3d per week.

Our neighbour said that our lawn needs digging up and re-sowing next spring. So now you know, Darling! You know, I shall be glad to have a man of my own around, for sometimes I get a bit fed up with the well-intentioned advice of other people's husbands. I think I am known as the grass-widow of Westfield Road!

We went on Beverley Westwood yesterday afternoon and Michael was accompanied by his imaginary baby sister. Once he tripped up and was most concerned because we did not pick the baby up!

Barbara had again been to visit her brother and his four daughters:

He cooked us a lovely tea. He is not going back to sea yet as the skipper and crew have all got the sack, due to some fault or other when they sailed. He bought Michael a lovely plastic car.

On June 12th, John wrote:

Only another month and I shall be home, and what's more I should be with you. We shall be loading at Bahrain tomorrow and once we have passed through the Canal we should know our port of destination. By the way, I have sent in my letter requesting leave whether the ship goes to the UK or the continent, just to be on the safe side. The crew seem to be working dead slow and none of them want overtime, so I don't know how I shall manage to smarten the ship up. I am afraid she will come to the UK looking the rust-box she is. We are carrying a cargo of Motor Spirit so that will put an end to all my efforts at removing rust, as it precludes the use of steel tools. I am afraid this is a very short letter as it is nearly 10pm and I have to be up before 4 in the morning, I just want to tell you that I love you with my whole being, and even though my letters are rather scarce, my thoughts of you aren't.

Barbara wrote:

This time I am trying not to get too excited about seeing you until I know your definite orders, as we have been so often disappointed, but as each day passes, I feel it is one nearer to being with you, dearest. I hope that in twenty-two days' time I shall not need to write to tell you I love you.

On June 28th, John wrote:

Soon we shall be starting on the last leg of our trip and by the time you receive this letter we should be well on our way home. We should be arriving at Suez tonight, so we hope we shall be going through in tomorrow's convoy.

The ship still looks like a rust-box from top to bottom. I painted the deck, but the next four or five days we shipped water on the deck, making it look as bad as ever. Then I coated all the rigging with white lead and tallow, and that night we had a sandstorm which made all the white turn a dirty brown colour. Now I am resigned to the ship getting home in this state, for I have very little paint left to cover all the rusty streaks and of course very little time to do it in.

No doubt I shall get a severe dressing down when we reach home, but if that is all I shall be lucky. In spite of this, I am looking forward intensely to reaching the UK and I can't wait to see you and Michael. Little did we think last July that we would be parted for another year. Until that happy time when I can give you my love in person, I want to send you lots and lots of love and kisses. Also, a big hug for Daddy's big boy.

In Barbara's final letter, she writes:

Probably next weekend at this time I shall know which port you are going to, and then it will not seem much longer until we are on our way to meet you. Michael has it all worked out how we are going to get there, even to having dinner on the train. He loves travelling about and being important. Do you remember our last night together, darling? Wasn't he a little horror! He still keeps on about Daddy bringing him a baby sister, so I tell him that he will have to wait until he is three – perhaps by then there will be one on the way.

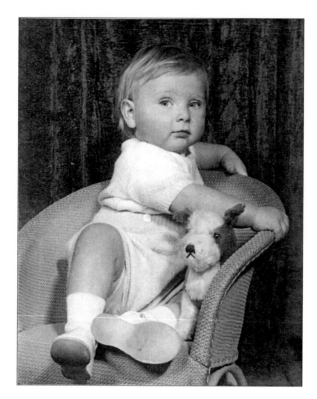

Michael's first birthday, January 1956

An angelic Michael with John's parents

Father and son on board ship, July 1956

Barbara's Christmas present to John   Brown but thin, Christmas 1956

CHAPTER SEVEN

SO NEAR AND YET SO FAR:
SEPTEMBER 1957 TO JUNE 1958

'Bye Bye Love'

After ten weeks together at home, Barbara was expecting another baby, but she was again writing to John:

> I am wondering whether you are now unpacking and settling in at your lodgings. Michael has asked several times 'What is Daddy doing now?'. When he went to bed, he asked where you were sleeping, so I said you would be in a little bed like him, and that seemed to please him.

John had enrolled on a lecturer-training course at Garnett College in London. This higher education college specialised in training people aged over 25, who were already qualified in their subject, to work in further or higher education. He travelled by train from Hull, changing at Doncaster, King's Cross and Balham, and then taking a taxi to his lodgings in Mount Ephraim Road, Streatham Hill South London:

> I was welcomed at No 42 by Jean, the landlady's daughter (no need to worry – she's about 40 and not my type!). I am sharing a room on the fourth floor (four storeys) with a boy from Leicester called Jack, who is also doing a course at Garnett College. His wife is expecting another baby either in March or April, so ours is the expectant fathers' room. There are however several other boys from the college staying here, including at least one taking nautical subjects. Also, several old ladies and a couple of elderly gentlemen. We had tea at 7 pm and it was a very good tea indeed. Apparently, the food here is very good and you can have as much as you want.

My room is quite nice with ample drawer space and as I arrived first I 'bagged' the bed near the window. The wash-place is on the next floor not far from our room, whilst the toilet is on the floor below. The room has a gas fire and gas ring, but of course we have to feed shillings into it to use it. Downstairs is a spacious lounge where we can study. The window looks down onto the gardens and lawn, which are very well kept indeed. Our room is quite big and quite well-furnished, but the lounge is absolutely chock-a-block with bric-a-brac of every description.

Apparently, we are allowed two baths a week for free, but we have to pay if we want more. We are called in the morning at 7.15 and have breakfast half an hour later, so that we arrive at college before 9.15, which is the time the lectures start. The college pays for our bus fares, which cost 6d each way, and each journey occupies just over fifteen minutes.

I won't be able to use the phone here, so I shall have to look around to see where the nearest phone box is. I am already missing you, dearest, and I shall be looking forward to six weeks' time when I shall be seeing you again. By the way, I think it might be an idea for me to come home by bus at half-term, as I expect it will be a good deal cheaper.

Take care of yourself my sweetheart and don't worry about me at any time. Give Michael a big kiss from Daddy and give my love to Mother and Dad at Beverley and at Hessle. Above all remember that I love, love, love, love you and that you are the most precious and sweet wife anyone could have.

'That'll Be the Day'

Back home, Michael had a new game:

It is called 'Going to College'. His rocker is the train, and he has two cases, like Daddy, and the small coloured towel like yours. I have to kiss him and then wave 'Bye-bye', and in less than half an hour we start all over again.

I cannot see you paying for an extra bath – I bet you think two a week is quite enough! I am enclosing your pants with this letter, so I hope you do not open it at the breakfast table.

John had now started at the college:

We are to do a lot of visiting, spending on average three afternoons a week either at nautical schools or other places of interest associated with our future work. There are only six of us in the Nautical Subjects section and I am the only one with Extra-Masters ticket. Apparently, the selection is rather strict after all, for of the students who went up to be interviewed at the same time as myself, only one was accepted. When we do our first lectures ourselves, two of us will be teaching at the London Nautical school, three at the King Edward VII Nautical School and one of at HMS Worcester. There are about 130 students at the college and about the same number of men as women. By the way, all the nautical types are married.

There does not appear to be a half-term, and I can't see any possibility of me being able to start travelling until teatime on a Friday as we have practice lessons on Fridays. There may be a little more leeway on Monday mornings.

The meals at the school are very good, although the dining hall is a little crowded when we are all in it at the same time. We have coffee and biscuits in the morning and tea and cakes in the afternoon – all on the house. Yesterday after tea we had a walk round the district, finishing up by having a beer and a game of darts at a local pub. We did locate a launderette quite close, charging 2/9 per 7lb load of washing so I may be visiting it at the weekend.

My day is certainly a full one, but that doesn't stop me thinking about you. However, I feel that I shall get a good deal out of this course and that it is hastening the time when we shall be together for good.

Barbara replied that it would not be practical for John to come home by coach for a weekend:

You would not get home until after 7pm on the Saturday and would have to leave again at 9.30 am on the Sunday, as there is only one coach a day. Whereas if you come home by train on the Friday evening and return overnight on the Sunday you will have practically 48 hours at home.

They were living on a grant while John was studying in London, so funds were rather tight. John wrote:

I think I should be able to manage on £25 per term, including my fares at the beginning and end of each term and at half term. I want to save enough out of it too, so that I can make your housekeeping up from £3-15-0 to £5 when

I am at home. This evening after phoning you, we all had half a pint at the local pub before returning to the digs. Small expenses such as that tend to build up during the week and I found I spent 30/- during my first week here. Of course, I have a refund of some of my bus fares to collect from college. Most of our odd shillings go into the gas meter and we find that is our single most expensive item. Our room, being at the top of the house and having a northerly aspect, tends to get very cold if we don't have the gas fire on in the evenings and 1/- only seems to last a night.

Barbara also gave an account of her expenditure:

Not only have I managed on the £3-15-0 this week, but I have 6d left! Actually, though, I would have spent about 5/- over, but my milk tokens came through this morning, and they were from the beginning of September, so I gave the milkman five tokens this week, and had only 1/5d to pay. Apart from bus fares, and the papers, all the money has gone on food, so I shall have to cut down a bit more to pay for shoe repairs etc.

Although John was used to doing his laundry (or 'dhobi') on board ship, Barbara felt he might need some advice:

Where do you wash your non-iron shirts – in the bathroom? I hope you did not take them to the launderette too.

John replied:

In future I shall endeavour not to send the non-iron items.

'My Special Angel'

He had sent his washing to the launderette with one of his house-mates, having been struck down by the flu. He seems however to have been well cared for:

Friday morning when I awoke I didn't feel at all special, so I thought it would be better to have a day in bed. Jean (the landlady's daughter) kept me well supplied with tea, Bovril, soup, coffee and suchlike, whilst on Thursday evening I had bought a bottle of Lucozade which I found very enjoyable. During Friday morning I sweated a good deal and by the afternoon I felt good enough to get up for a while. Friday evening though I developed a sore throat and on Saturday morning I could hardly speak. Anyhow it started improving then and by the afternoon my voice had returned, and I got up for a couple of hours. One of the other students brought me in a bottle of lemon barley which I find most refreshing.

Back home, various members of Barbara's family were also unwell:

When we went over to Hessle this afternoon, I found Mother was really very poorly and Dad was not too grand, but he went to work. Apparently, they have a lot of drivers off sick, and Dad has been working overtime every day. Mother said one night he was only in bed 3½ hours. I shall not be surprised to hear in the morning that Dad is confined to bed too.

She hoped John's parents had not succumbed too:

Actually, they have a good chance of missing the flu, as they do not mix with others much, do they?

In fact, not only did John's parents catch the flu, but so did Barbara and Michael, leaving Barbara with a lingering cough. The Asian flu epidemic affected nine million people in the UK and caused six hundred deaths during one week in October. John wrote:

One of the others has not been at college the last few days so we are wondering whether he has the flu or whether he has become discouraged. My discouragement starts tomorrow when we begin our speech training and on Tuesday when we start on English.

A few days later he wrote,

So far, we have dodged the speeches, but we must make a start on Friday. We have essays and problems to make up every fortnight, and much of the remainder is Educational Psychology and Philosophy.

I received my first essays back after marking. The first was marked C and the second B, so even if the standard is a bit low it has improved a little. On Friday we have to take our first lesson and we shall be having it recorded so that we can check for faults in speech and presentation.

We had our first Students' Assembly on Friday, under our president. In it, I let myself in for a job assisting in the library, whilst I have entered myself in the groups for tennis, table tennis, cricket, swimming, football and debating. I am wondering which groups will mature.

'Whole lotta Woman'

Meanwhile, Barbara's pregnancy was becoming increasingly apparent:

Even Mother said she thinks it must be a little elephant this time. I am more than ever convinced that it is at least triplets. I shall have to do some 'foundation' shopping in the next week or so, as my others are getting really tight.

Barbara was tempted to tell Michael that his long-awaited baby brother or sister was finally on the way, but decided against it:

After all, six months is a long time for a child to wait, isn't it? After tea, Michael and I sorted out some of the snaps of him, to put in his Baby Book. He did not believe that the earliest ones were him, and said they were his baby cousin. He probably does not understand that everyone starts as a tiny baby but will accept it more easily when he can watch his own brother or sister grow.

Michael has had his first lessons in Geography this week. He started asking why the sun comes out in daytime and the moon comes out at night. Then he wanted to know where they were when they were not here. So, I explained about other countries like Australia having their daytime when we are in bed etc. Isn't it amazing how soon they want to know these things? For some reasons, I am glad we have not had a second baby too soon, for it means I can give so much more time to answering Michael's questions, which probably compensates him for the lack of his own 'playmate'.

We had the radio on this morning, but when I turned it on at tea-time, nothing happened. Michael said he has not touched it, and I do not think he has, so what do you think will be the matter? Michael says that Daddy knows how to mend it, implying that I am a bit dim.

In his next letter, John sent detailed instructions on how to mend the radio:

I think the fault with the radio will be a wire which has come off the volume control. The set must be unplugged at the mains plug before you touch it though. You first take the cardboard sheet off the bottom of the set and if you examine the back of the volume control you will see it is something as follows: (Here he included a labelled diagram). I think the trouble will be that either wire (a) or wire (b) has come off its respective tag as they are not soldered on.

If you make a hook at the end of the wire and then poke it on with a small screwdriver it may do the trick, but you have to be very careful not to break any wire adrift at the same time for they are very brittle. When I come home next I can have a go at soldering them.

Barbara attempted to follow the instructions, but then decided to leave the job to John, who managed a weekend at home before starting his teaching practice. This was to take place on the HMS Worcester, moored off Greenhithe on the River Thames since 1871, along with other ships now being used for nautical training. John arranged to stay with Barbara's sister, Joan, who had moved to army quarters at Gravesend in Kent, and Barbara and Michael would join him there. Barbara wrote:

Joan said we shall need all our winter woollies down there, as the winds are very keen, so if you have not already changed into your winter vests darling, you had better take them with you.

I must have swallowed a balloon over the weekend, for I have filled out ever so much, overnight. My clothes are all a tight fit today, so I shall have to go into my maternity skirts permanently now. I have spent this evening altering my grey maternity skirt. It always was rather long, and now that skirts are worn shorter, it looked excessively so. I am just four months, so I should 'quicken' in the next week or so, certainly some time while we are at Joan's. I am carrying this baby exactly as I carried Michael – all round – so it must be another boy!

After spending three weeks together at Gravesend, Barbara returned home, and John went back to his lodgings. Barbara wrote:

Yesterday and today have seemed rather unreal, as though I expected you to walk in any time, but I expect I shall soon settle in the old routine again.

Back in London, John took advantage of a free Wednesday afternoon to visit the Houses of Parliament and to sit in on debates in both Houses. He was also improving his own speaking skills:

On Thursday we had our first speech training lessons, so if you find me looking in a mirror and making queer shapes with my mouth and tongue when I come home, give me time to explain before you get me certified.

On another free Wednesday afternoon, John and his companions went to the Old Bailey and sat in at a court case there:

A woman QC was conducting the defence and it appeared to be masterly and effective. In certain respects, though, the case was a little gruesome, but I thought it was a valuable experience.

In the evening I went to the library where I looked at various books on Divorce. Don't get worried – I have to lead a discussion group on Tuesday at the college, and the subject is whether divorce should be made harder or easier.

'Let's Have a Ball'

John and his fellow lodgers had a rather extended night out:

On Thursday evening, the four of us were invited to the 'Down Under' club by the nurse at the digs. The club was way over in Chelsea, so it was after 8.30 before we reached it. A concert was being given there by a famous Australian artist – mainly songs accompanied with a piano-accordion. The songs were mostly borderline cases but were quite good. Of course, there was plenty of beer to be had but very little room and I have never seen so many people crowd into two small rooms like that before. The audience were practically all Australians or New Zealanders, so of course not all the songs were complimentary to the Mother Country, but at the same time songs were sung criticising Australia, and the general spirit was very good.

We left sometime about half past eleven and then hunted around for somewhere to have a cup of coffee. Eventually we found a café open, so we had the coffee and then hunted around for a way back to the digs. We decided to go by Underground but to our dismay the last train had just gone. Of course, the bus service stops about midnight, but we saw one bus coming along bound for Victoria, so we hopped on there. At Victoria we hoped to get a steam train to Streatham Hill, but here too the station was closed. Anyhow, on enquiry we were told that if we walked down to the embankment we could catch a bus there. Well, our sense of direction couldn't have been very good, for our trek took us past Buckingham Palace, down the Mall and then along Whitehall. As we went by St James's Park, I thought of another early morning when you and I had watched the sun rise not far from where we were then.

After we reached the Mall we had not long to wait before a bus came along and by changing buses we were soon back at the digs. We finally got in just after 2 am. It had been an enjoyable night, but rather costly, and I wished you could have been with me rather than the other lads.

He finished his letter with three rows of kisses:

xxxxxxxxxx to the dearest most beautiful and sweetest wife anyone could have

xxxxxxxxxx to Scampy

xxxxxxxxxx to David or Hazel or them both

Barbara meanwhile was wondering whether to make a frilled petticoat for the baby:

I certainly shan't need one if it is another boy. Some days I feel I wish I knew the baby's sex, and other days I am not at all bothered. The other day when I told Michael not to jump on the chairs, he retorted that when the baby comes he will teach 'it' to jump on the chairs as well. Can you imagine a fortnight old baby bouncing on the chairs, darling? It is amazing the things our baby is going to be taught by his/her older brother.

She continued:

What a lot has happened since we watched the sunrise in St James's Park. We have so many happy memories to share.

Michael tells everyone that you will soon be home, and the number of times he asks me how many more days there are to wait. I have promised him that, providing you come on the earlier train, he can sit up until you come home – if he does not wreck the house anymore!

I suppose I really must go to bed now, so until Friday when we shall be together again, all my love and kisses to my Beloved. God bless and sweet dreams.

Oh Boy!

After a family Christmas back in Hull, his first Christmas with Barbara since 1953, John returned to Garnett College. On the day he travelled down to London, his grant of £89-10-6 arrived from the Education Committee.

Barbara wrote her first letter to him, after spending the evening knitting a vest for the new baby. The next day she had a worrying moment:

I had dressed Michael ready to go out and had only my dress and coat to put on, so I opened the front door and let him put out the milk-bottles. I heard him chatting to the Co-op milkman whilst I finished getting ready, so I was surprised to find he was not in the front when I went out. I thought he must have wandered down the back, so I dashed round calling to him. Our neighbour heard me and said she had seen him on Sunbeam Road, so I ran off to the top and saw his Lordship waiting at the corner of Belgrave Drive. He just waved when I called and stood laughing until I caught up to him. Then he said he was 'just walking on a bit' and that he had 'waited to let the cars go by'. He certainly gave me a scare, and I have tried to impress on him that he must always wait for me, but I shall be extra careful in future.

It turned out that Michael had decided to visit Barbara's mother, his Nanna. Barbara was surprised to find that he knew not only which bus to catch but also her mother's full address. It turned out that he had learnt it from Beauty, his Nanna's budgerigar, which had been trained to repeat its address in case it went missing.

John was living the high life in London, as one of the lodgers had a kettle in his room and had bought a teapot:

We generally have a cup of tea each evening before we go to bed plus odd cups at other times. In fact, at the rate we have used up our first quarter of tea, it will be a costly business. Crosswords have been our relaxation this week, and we have sent two off to the newspapers in the hope of earning a guinea or two.

When he came home at Christmas, Barbara had found lipstick marks on his pyjamas. John wrote:

I haven't mentioned about the marks on the pyjamas, but none of the boys have said anything so I don't think they could have been behind it.

Barbara replied:

If the boys are not responsible for the lipstick marks, it rather points to Jean, doesn't it? Has she made any overtures yet, darling? I must say I am curious, but definitely not worried, for I trust you and have faith in you.

John replied:

Jean hasn't made any overtures yet, so I am still ignorant of the cause of the pyjama marks. It wouldn't matter how many overtures I received though – there would still be only one girl for me – YOU.

'La Dee Dah'

He was preparing to start his teaching practice at Southampton:

I can see that I shall have to polish up both my presentation and my subject matter. The speech training teacher pulled me up the other day for speaking in too high a voice, so I will have to speak down in my boots.

Meanwhile he had received B- for his last essay, together with a comment on his poor spelling. Barbara commented:

Do you think carelessness is the cause of your spelling mistakes, or are you using long words which you are not sure of? By the way, SEPARATION (A not E).

John replied:

Thanks for the spelling tip, bring any other mistakes to my notice that you see.

He next had to write an essay with the title: 'A clash of doctrines is not a disaster, but a challenge'. He was awarded A for content, B- for English.

Barbara was unimpressed:

It seems your English still needs improving as B- is barely passable. Spelling mistake: PREFERABLE (E not A).

Before starting his teaching practice, he had to deliver a practice lecture:

I don't think it was quite as bad as my last one – but it still wasn't good. It engendered a good deal of criticism. The teacher appeared more satisfied with my pronunciation when I spoke in a high pitch and less satisfied with the pitch when my pronunciation was all right. Now I have to combine the two.

John decided it was time for some rest and recuperation:

'Who's sorry now?'

Don, Dick and I decided to try our feet at ice skating. We went down to Streatham ice rink and lined up a pair of skates and then had a go. It wasn't too bad, Don soon got the hang of it, but I'm afraid my efforts were a bit amateurish – although at times spectacular. We spent about an hour or so at the rink and after I had picked myself off the ice for the ninth or tenth time we staggered off the rink and back to the digs. Now I am feeling the after-effects of the exercise – my ankles feel like a pair of ball-bearings and I have various aches and pains in other parts of my anatomy. It will be some little time before I have another shot at skating – some less strenuous form of exercise will do.

Barbara replied:

You sound as though you did as well as I did the one and only time I went to the roller-skating rink. I spent more time on my 'sit-upon' than on my feet. However, I hope by now you are recovering from your bumps and bruises. (By the way, darling, APPARENTLY is spelt with two As and one E).

Meanwhile, she was keeping the home fires burning:

I ordered some more coal today as our stock is very low and I do not want to run out. Despite using coke, I think we are using more than the allowance, so I shall have to keep an eye on it, as we shall need a fire through the summer for the baby, at least until after bath-time each day. I think it is possible to get off-ration coal, though, if necessary.

It has been a very cold day here, and since tea-time a gale has been blowing, so I am glad to be inside. Even so, the draughts have pervaded the house, and I think bed with a hot-water-bottle will be the warmest place.

The next day, she wrote:

It is almost too cold to write tonight, so if my writing is even worse than usual, you will know it is because my hand is shivering! Once again, I'm almost sitting in the fireplace in an attempt to get warm. Despite a good fire it is bitterly cold, so I'm wondering how you are faring darling, with only a gas fire.

John replied:

We have had very slight falls of snow here. To keep warm, all four of us usually spend the evening in one room with the gas fire on. However, the beds are not as cold now as when we first came down, and in any case, we always put our top coats over the blankets to keep the warmth in.

He was however thinking of splashing out on a new overcoat:

Jean asked all of us at the lodgings whether we wanted to buy an overcoat which a friend has given her to sell for £15. It is a second-hand one but hasn't been worn a lot and it appears to be a very good quality. I tried it on and it fits me perfectly. In spite of the price I think it would be a good buy and it would last a good number of years. I expect I shall be needing a new overcoat as the one I have is hardly suitable for me when I get a job. Let me know what you think and if you think it would be worth it I could bring the money back when I come home. I know it is hardly the time really when I want to be buying things like that but let me know what you think. The overcoat is dark grey – not over attractive in colour but it should be very serviceable.

Back in Hull, a heavily pregnant Barbara was experiencing restless nights from *'our over energetic baby who does not seem to rest at all'*. She had lost two more teeth during this pregnancy and was suffering from varicose veins. She was also feeling downhearted about the toll that pregnancy was taking on her personal appearance:

My hairdresser said that the baby has taken the life out of my hair this time and advised me to try a lanolin shampoo. Remembering how I lost my hair when feeding Michael, I will take her advice. I do not want to be bald as well as gummy.

She continued:

This baby of ours is just about wearing me out. It is never still during the day and sometimes I feel really tired and sick with it constantly moving. I shall be ready for a rest in the nursing home after baby's born! Today Michael wanted to know what we will call it if it is just a baby. Try as I could, he would not be convinced that it will be either a baby boy or a baby girl. He kept saying 'Well, it might be just a baby!'

Whilst waiting for the baby, Barbara was busy sewing:

This morning I bought some tape for the necks of the nighties, and Michael told the lady in the shop that it was 'for my baby's nighties that my mummy is making'. I think it is the first time he's mentioned the baby to a stranger, he still considers it our secret. Did I tell you Michael has decided he is going to go to college when he is a big boy? He said he will write to me, and telephone 'like Daddy does'.

'Alone'

She was missing John:

When I look back and think we went over a year without seeing each other, with only occasional letters, I wonder how I ever survived. The past three weeks seem to have dragged by, and I'm longing to be with you again my darling. I'm especially looking forward to the Easter holiday, and I do hope you will be at home when the baby is born.

John wrote:

It was lovely to hear from you, but I wish you could be with me here. It seems queer that a month down on this course away from you should seem as long as a year away at sea and yet I do seem to miss you much more when I know that I could pop on the train on Friday night and came over to see you. Still I suppose I must wait another three weeks before I come, for the more often that I am with you, the more often I want to be with you.

Barbara had shocked John's parents by smacking Michael when he misbehaved in front of them. John supported her:

I quite agree with you that sometimes Michael does need a slap and it is as well for him to know that he can't misbehave when his grandparents are there. I don't want him to think he will get special treatment when he's at his grandparents. At Easter, if I am looking after him, I want to keep his discipline as much as possible like it is when you are at home.

In February, John moved to Southampton University to start his four-week spring term teaching practice at the Navigation School. His accommodation was provided:

The room is very nice: a desk, fair-sized bed (room for you), wardrobe, gas fire (takes shillings), and attached room having wash basin and hot and cold water. However, the bugle wakes me up at 6:30 am although breakfast is not until 8:30. The food here is very good indeed – much above the Garnet College standard.

The subjects he had to teach the cadets included ship construction, physics, maths, seamanship, chart-work, meteorology, cargo-work, electricity and legal knowledge:

It would appear that I shall be taking three classes daily, so I should be kept fully occupied in preparing lessons. Some days I will be off for barely half an hour whilst on the best day I have one and a half hours for preparation. The first two weeks should be teaching in the junior department but the second two weeks will be at the senior department.

This school seems to be run on a slightly higher standard than the Worcester, but perhaps that is possible because all the cadets are over 16. Also, I consider the connection between the junior and senior sides is a good thing. An advantage which this school has over all the other nautical schools is its connection with the University. Hence, things haven't to be done on the cheap – as so often occurs in other schools. There seems to be a very good spirit between the Masters, and ready cooperation between the junior and senior sides. One snag I do find is having to salute back all the various cadets whenever I pass them.

'The Story of My Life'

Everything was going well until he started delivering lectures:

The first lesson didn't go down too bad as I used one of the Worcester lessons. However, the second lecture I took – one on Mechanical Design – was hopeless. Unluckily for me, the head of the junior department was in there listening to me. I failed to take into account the size of the room (two rooms in one), hence the blackboard work was illegible before you had gone halfway down the length of the room. My drawings also went haywire, as it is a subject I have never taken before. I wonder how I shall fare the next lesson in that subject next week.

Like any trainee-teacher, John had to receive feedback on his teaching. He was criticised for 'atrocious blackboard work and layout' and for his pronunciation. However, the feedback also said that it was a 'difficult lecture handled in a competent manner' and commented on John's 'versatility and width of knowledge.' Barbara reassured him:

> Of course, blackboard work is a thing in which you will improve as you get more experience. I'm glad you impressed them with your knowledge, sweetheart. I always knew I had a very clever husband. Correction: LIKELIHOOD (I not Y).

The next week, John wrote:

> This week has been rather more hectic than last, and I have on average two lectures a day. Those I took in the early part of the week seemed to go all right but yesterday's weren't great. Perhaps it was due to my having to prepare three lectures yesterday. Anyhow by the time I had gathered the various information together I was only able to prepare very brief notes. The first lesson on Mathematics wasn't too bad but the next one on Seamanship was rather trying as I had two classes combined and the question and answers method I had prepared was not really suitable. The third period was on Geometry and I got in rather a mix-up on the board and was thankful to escape by giving them some problems.

He then moved to the Senior school:

> Both the head of the senior school and the head of the junior side were listening to them, so I had quite an audience. One of the lecturers afterwards said I didn't appear nervous – little did he know how I really felt. The first lecture was on Chart-work to the Second Mates and the second on Meteorology to the Masters. In both, the main criticism I received was that I was going too fast. My first lecture on Thursday morning was on electricity, dealing specifically with the composition of batteries and accumulators. It didn't go too badly but I got rather mixed up between charging and discharging accumulators. I had a short Rule of the Road period after Mr Evans arrived and he took the opportunity of watching it. Some of it went all right but when I started asking questions on how the ship was heading, I got mixed up according to whether they or I were on the ship.

I quite enjoyed today's lectures and I feel they went quite reasonably. Still I noticed my blackboard work was rather large and very scrappy. I shall have to prepare a rough plan of what I'm going to put on the blackboard beforehand. I do find teaching on the senior side more enjoyable than on the junior side. In the first place the students are usually quite eager to learn, and teaching them seems to give you much more satisfaction. Secondly the subjects themselves are that much more interesting as they are progressive rather than stagnant.

The trouble is that when I have three lectures or lessons in a day it takes me all evening to read up and prepare them, plus the period I have off at school. Of course, even for the regular lecturers, they find four periods is quite enough and they rarely do more during one day.

It was no wonder that John developed a smoking habit:

I find I am smoking quite heavily now (10 a week).

After finishing his teaching practice in Southampton, John came home for a weekend. The next day, Barbara wrote:

When Michael came into our bedroom this morning, he said 'Where's Daddy? Is he hiding?' I said you went back on the train last night while he was asleep, but you would be coming home in a few weeks' time.

A few days later, she wrote:

As you may have heard from the radio, we're really having some snow. Blizzards started yesterday afternoon and continued through the night. This morning the snow was well over a foot deep and I had to force the back door open when I wanted to get some coal. Then I dug a little path to the coal box and shelter before filling up the coal scuttle.

I thought I had a frost-bitten ear. I woke this morning with an awful pain in my left ear, and it was very red, with tiny white patches. I wrapped a scarf round my head when I went out this afternoon, But I suppose I should have done so yesterday. Michael says Jack Frost is very naughty for biting me.

The next day she continued:

Our neighbour said that if it was frostbite I would have no feeling in it, which I have, because it feels as though it is burning, so I went to see Dr Donaldson, and he says it is a sort of chilblain.

John's teaching practice continued with another four weeks at St John Cass Nautical College in London, teaching Navigational Aids to Masters and Mates. Although he had to lecture to groups of eighty, the timetable was much easier and there were more tutorials than lectures to deliver:

> *My lecture on electronic navigational aids wasn't much of a success. I'd made a mistake in my notes and when I repeated this on the board it got me in rather a muddle. The lecturer had to give me a hand to sort it out. Of course, it was a subject about which all my information has been gleaned from textbooks, and it is not as easy to teach this as it is to teach something you have practical experience of. On Thursday one of the Garnet College lecturers came to listen in on my meteorology lesson. I rather hurried the lesson, but it didn't go too bad and I think the lecturer was quite satisfied. Of course, the next fortnight is the period during which we are assessed so I expect I shall have more visitors.*

> *The main criticism I receive is still that I try to cram too much into one lecture. They seem to think the content of the lectures is good, but I give far more than the students can absorb. Anyhow I think my blackboard work has improved a bit.*

'Maybe Baby'

Meanwhile, Barbara was still planning to ask her doctor about the possibility that she was expecting twins:

> *I am sure there is more than one. Apart from the unending activity, I am a terrific size compared to when Michael was on the way.*

With his family increasing, John was pleased that his future employment seemed secure. He had been offered a post at the Hull Nautical College, next to the school on the Boulevard that he had joined in 1941 and left in 1944 to start his apprenticeship:

> *There have been no more vacancies in nautical schools, so the other lads are getting quite worried. With the rising unemployment figures I think it is going to be important to settle down in a steady job for a few years. I'm looking forward to finding out more about this job at the Boulevard. It should command a wage of over £800 a year I think (or at least I hope). Once I know for certain we shall be able to make our future plans.*

His teaching practice had ended on a positive note:

On Thursday I was quite bucked up with the comments of the regular lecturer who sat in to the lecture. I took the lecture rather more slowly than previously and he afterwards told me I had gone at just the right rate, had stressed just the right points and covered all the required ground.

He was now able to relax and enjoy himself. While there were still regular snow falls in Hull, the weather in London was warming up:

This morning we all went down to the tennis courts and spent about 1½ hours playing. I am feeling a bit stiff now, but I thoroughly enjoyed the game.

He would soon be home for the Easter holiday. Barbara wrote:

Do you realise, sweetheart, that on Thursday it will be five years since we met? This year I shall be looking forward to your homecoming, although the way I feel today, I should not be surprised if our baby arrives before you get home, darling. I wonder what our baby will be like. I hope he or she will be as good as Michael was, despite his or her present restlessness.

'I Love You Baby'

On April 22nd, John was back in London after his Easter holiday. He wrote:

I wonder whether you will still be at your mother's by the time this arrives there, or whether you are already in the nursing home. Wherever you are, you can rest assured that you are uppermost in my mind. I was hoping baby would arrive whilst I was home with you, but at least we were able to have the maximum time together. Even so, the holidays went by far too quickly.

The next day he was back on the train to Hull, having sent a telegram to Barbara:

THRILLED AND DELIGHTED DEAREST FONDEST LOVE COMING UP = JOHN

Michael finally had the little sister that he wanted, and Barbara had someone to make frilly petticoats for. After John's flying return visit, missing three days of college, he wrote:

It was lovely to be able to see you, Michael and Hazel for a few days, and I feel much more contented now, although of course I should have liked to have stayed with you longer. Later tonight I expect we shall be popping around to the Horse and Groom, as no doubt Hazel Barbara will have a number of well-wishers.

Barbara wrote to him from the nursing home. The birth had not been straightforward. Again, she was under a general anaesthetic for the birth, and she had suffered a postnatal haemorrhage. The new baby was not entirely angelic:

Hazel is a very dirty little girl, she's forever filling her pants, and today she had to have another complete change of clothing. Last night she soaked not only me but also my bed, so I had to sleep on a wet bed – your daughter!! I am sure she seems to be filling out though, and must have a strong back, as already she can raise her head away from my shoulder, which is good going for only one week. I hope she is as easy to bring up as Michael.

As well as giving news of Hazel's progress, Barbara described a slightly bizarre incident:

We had a very eventful night last night. During the early hours I was awakened suddenly by an unusual noise. As we put the lights on, we found there had been a heavy fall of soot in the fireplace. We settled down again, but 10 minutes later there was another funny noise, and the sound of something dropping from the ceiling. On investigation, we found a bird had come down the chimney, and brought another cloud of soot. Our movements disturbed the bird, and it flew frantically round the room – while we hid under the bed clothes! However, the nurse soon came in answer to our urgent summons. She succeeded in catching the sparrow and put it out. But what a panic – I thought I should not sleep any more but dropped off fairly quickly.

The next few days were not the best of times for Barbara:

Yesterday the American girl was moved into our room and has rather shattered the peaceful atmosphere. For the first two hours she continuously criticised the nursing home, nurses, the doctor and the attention she has been given, and since then has criticised England, English products, way of life etc. We had the elderly nurse on again last night. It appears she is 69 and the matron's older sister. However now I am up a little, I am not dependent on her coming to wash me, thank goodness. Now it is visiting time, and I am just about going mad with longing for you, dearest. The other two girls have their husbands here and they are being most affectionate, so you can imagine how I am feeling.

But there were some lighter moments:

We had a good laugh this evening. Sister brought the babies about 5:30 pm and a short while later we saw her down the garden feeding the pigs! An hour later she came to collect the babies and sat chatting to us with a baby tucked under each arm, and she was quite oblivious to the fact that one was streaming down her. Our daughter managed to fill her pants again, but this time not on me.

Meanwhile in London, John had suffered a minor injury:

The other day the Garnett College cricket team assembled for its first practice game on Tooting Bec Common. It was a lovely day and we all enjoyed the game. However, for a couple of days I have been limping about, the results of a cricket ball hitting my left instep. Today the swelling has gone down and all the pain has ceased and once more I can walk about normally.

Barbara replied:

I hope your foot is better now – I always have thought cricket a dangerous game! We are home again, and it is lovely to be here with Michael. Now we only need you to come to complete our little family.

'It's Too Soon to Know'

She had been the registry office to register Hazel's birth:

When he asked me your occupation, I said 'teacher', but then he asked for further details: primary, grammar, further education etc and said that the statistical department needed the detailed information. So, I said you were at a Nautical College and hoped he would not ask which one. However, that satisfied him, and he looked it up in his classified list and then said the correct description was 'lecturer', so that is what he put down. I felt quite flustered for a few minutes, so much so that when he asked me the baby's name, I said, 'Barbara Hazel' and then had to correct myself before he wrote it down.

When Hazel was weighed, I was delighted to see she was 9 pounds, so she has gained 10 ounces above her birth weight. Mother said it is hard to believe she is not a fortnight old yet, as she looks so plump and moves her head so well.

John had been on an outing with Don, Dick and Dave:

It was almost 10 by the time we reached Purley, so we only called at a couple of pubs. I thought it was perhaps just as well, as Dave had to drive us back. The first pub we called at had the bar decorated with model sailing ships whilst an adjacent bar room was decorated with model stagecoaches. The chief virtues of the second pub were the outside table and chairs and also its later closing time – 11 pm. We had really quite a pleasant time as it was a lovely warm evening. However, I would much rather have spent the evening out with you. Roll on Whitsun when I will be home once more. I am looking forward to seeing all my family at home. Doesn't our family seem more complete to you now that there is Hazel to attend to?

Hazel continued much as she had started. Barbara wrote:

I let her have another kick in her pram before her 6pm feed but she shocked Michael when she dirtied the nappy she was lying on, and then rubbed her feet in it – Michael's face was a picture. She does not like being bathed though and yelled all the time I was seeing to her.

Michael is being very good with Hazel, but she is having to get used to some hard kisses. Still, they say babies can stand rough handling, so I do not interfere too much, as he is just a little touchy about criticism.

John clearly thought that Hazel was going to be a handful:

You will need to get a folding pram and I feel that Hazel will need a robust one.

In London there was a bus strike, but his friend Dave had come to the rescue with his car:

Dave picks us up each morning and runs us to the college. We have to start off a little earlier and the car barely crawls through the city but we generally get there in time. Not so the first day when we abandoned the car near London Bridge and arrived one hour late. My foot seems to have fully recovered. In fact, I walked about 1½ miles the other day from the nearest tube station to the lodgings, and in so doing beat the other two who I left in the city to come back by car. I was back at the digs more than five minutes before them.

As usual, Barbara was visiting her family with the new baby:

Mother thinks Hazel is very much like me as a baby, Joyce said she is like Michael, but personally I can see no likeness to either Michael or myself. I think she is much more like you! Already she seems to take an interest in things, and she seems particularly quick at picking out Michael's voice. As soon as he speaks, she turns her head and her little eyes follow him around.

I felt quite annoyed with Joyce this afternoon. She persistently teased Michael and pretended she was going to take Hazel, until he was almost in tears. Consequently, when Mother started to walk back with the pram, Michael cried heartbrokenly, as he thought she was taking his precious little sister away from him. I was quite a while before I would get him to understand Nanna was only taking her part of the way home for us, and that no one will take Hazel away from us. Michael has been so good about baby too – it seems such a shame that he should be upset.

John meanwhile had been attending a course on radar:

The course at Sir John Cass has been quite interesting, and on Thursday we went for a trip up the river as far as Southend on the radar training launch. Unfortunately, we were cooped up in a classroom most of the time but what we did see of the banks and traffic on the Thames was impressive and most interesting. Next week we are once again attending the radar course and towards the end of the week we shall be examined. I don't intend doing any swotting for this exam as I am more concerned with the end of term college exams. What reading I am doing in the evenings is educational rather than technical.

But he was still finding time to relax:

'A Wonderful Time Up There'

Yesterday we had quite a pleasant day. In the morning as usual we took our washing along and then called in at the library to change our books. Straight after lunch we caught a train to Eltham Park where we were playing King Edward VII Nautical College at cricket. I wasn't on the team but as our side was one man short I joined in. I didn't score any runs but at least I was still not out at the end of the match so it wasn't so bad. In any case our team achieved an easy victory so it was a successful venture. The cricket field was in the middle of the park, on the edge of a wood filled with bluebells. Tea was laid on so it was a very enjoyable afternoon. In the evening Don, Dick and I went out to a couple of local pubs and had a drink at each (ostensibly to celebrate my income tax rebate). However we were back by 10 PM and had a relatively early night.

Barbara commented:

Congratulations on not getting a 'duck' on Saturday, darling. I can see you will be quite a sportsman when you come home! Don't you find it a pleasant change after being at sea?

She was dismayed to find that she was again losing her hair:

When I washed my hair tonight, I found it is coming out in handfuls, so I may go to see the doctor and get a tonic.

However, she cheered herself up by going on a shopping spree:

For Michael I bought some white sand-shoes for playing in, a white T-shirt, ankle socks, and material to make two shirts for afternoons. For Hazel I bought some nylon and some lace edging to make her some frilly petticoats, and for myself I bought shoes, a handbag and stockings. The shoes are very fashionable black suede ones with the new pointed toe.

Hazel must have been a noisy baby, because John wrote:

Does Michael take a dim view of Hazel's ability to raise the roof? I think I'll buy myself a pair of earplugs before I come home at Whitsun.

Barbara replied:

Hazel's crying (!!) does not seem to bother Michael very much, except that he always wants me to pick her up straight away, but I have explained that babies have to cry sometimes as it helps them to grow. (If the noise is anything to go by, Hazel will be a big girl!!). She seems to sleep better during the day if I wrap her up well and put her outside in the pram. This evening I have been sewing Hazel's petticoats and I have really enjoyed doing it. It is lovely making things for our daughter, instead of other people's.

John was now working hard for his exams, most of the time:

> We haven't been out anywhere this week apart from the college. However, during the lunch hour we find it most entertaining to go down to Tower Hill and there to listen to the various orators telling the world at large their views of the world and of destiny. I may go down to Tooting Bec Common on Saturday with the other boys to play tennis. My foot seems to be back to normal now.

'On the Street Where You Live'

John came home for a week at Whitsuntide and then returned to London to prepare for his exams:

> At college we have been doing quite a lot of reading, although on Friday we spent all afternoon carrying out experiments in the laboratory. Yesterday we went to the London Planetarium, which we found interesting but perhaps not so educating as we thought it might be. We arrived at the planetarium about 2 pm but found it did not open until 3:30 so I paid a visit to Madame Tussaud's which was next door. Have you been there dearest? It helped to pass an hour away and was quite interesting.

They resumed their regular three-minute telephone calls, sometimes interrupted by the operator and sometimes by the children. Barbara wrote:

> It was lovely to hear from you this evening darling, though it seemed a very hectic three minutes. Michael was very fussy that he had been able to talk to you on your birthday and he is eager to know whether you like your present. Hazel was keeping an offended silence when I went to pick her up again, but she was soon giggling happily again.

Family planning had never been a concern when John was away at sea, but Barbara was now thinking ahead:

> I am told that one has to wait six months before going to the birth control clinic, so what do you suggest we do? I feel we should take some precautions, as we do not want to start another baby so soon, if at all. The 'you-know-what's do seem rather expensive – it looks as though it will have to be an occasional luxury in future!!!

Her doctor had advised her against increasing their family further:

Although it would not be actually dangerous for me to have another baby, he advises us not to, as I shall have the same trouble and it is very weakening. Apparently, I suffer from inertia of the womb, which causes long labours, and a delay in the contraction of the womb immediately following the baby's birth. This is what caused the heavy haemorrhage I had this time. In addition, the afterbirth always breaks up instead of coming out whole, and I have again retained a fraction of it.

Meanwhile, she was thinking about sending Michael to Sunday school:

I feel he is ready to go now, and it would perhaps counteract this showing-off business, which has developed since Hazel was born. What do you think, darling?

Maybe Michael was jealous of the attention the new baby was receiving:

Hazel seems so cuddly, which is her great appeal, I think. I am afraid our little daughter gets rather more nursing than Michael did, but she seems to like it more. She is rather nattery unless she is being wheeled or nursed. Maybe she just likes cuddles, like her mother!

I had a good laugh at Hazel last night. I had apparently disturbed her when I went to bed, and when I put the lights on, she was laid there laughing and nodding and shaking her head, as though she was having a conversation with someone, she did look funny.

Michael also had his moment to shine, however. Barbara sent John a photograph of Michael and Beauty the budgerigar. His photograph had been taken by the Hull Daily Mail in connection with the incident that had happened earlier in the year and which Barbara's mother had mentioned to a contact at the newspaper:

First of all, Michael did not want to be photographed, then when we had talked him round, the bird would not cooperate. I am surprised the photograph came out so well.

She concluded her letter:

I am missing you terribly and next Thursday cannot come quick enough for me. It is rather strange, considering the length of time you have been away, but since Easter I have been quite miserable about being separated from you, darling. Yet I have had plenty to occupy me. It is just that I long for you so much, sweetheart.

John was not entirely confident about his performance in the exams:

We have had two exams so far and I think I may have managed to scrape through. Still I don't know how they are marked, for I hardly managed to give any facts – I just talked about nothing in connection with each question for 45 minutes. I suppose I will lose a good few marks over my English which in conjunction with my spelling really was poor. Anyhow I think they mark generously and tomorrow we have the health paper to come.

'Rave on'

Eventually the last exam was over:

Don, Dick, two of the other boys and myself celebrated the end of our exams by visiting Chelsea and calling at a few of the public houses there. We certainly saw some 'types' and finally settled down in a little pub, where there was a band and communal singing. When closing time came along we had to make a dash for the last tube – catching it with only seconds to spare.

The next day they were invited to a party in Finchley:

We went along to the party armed with a small supply of full beer bottles. Apparently, some of the Garnett students had cleared their apartment of furniture and had laid on supplies of light refreshments, liquor and a jukebox. We found the party rather crowded as I suppose there were about 40 people there. However, an amateur skiffle group had been formed from the guests and there was music, dancing and drinking! All through the evening I kept wishing that I could have been with you rather than at the party – although it would have been hardly the type of party we should have chosen. Anyway, by and by the beer ran out, the music stopped, and we left by tube for the digs.

I bet by now you are thinking that your husband is a regular imbiber, but I can assure you my glass generally lasts a long while. However, I felt myself that two nights running is a bit hectic, but I expect that will do us for the course – apart from perhaps an odd drink at the college dance. It is a matter of keeping in the group, but it doesn't appeal to me as a pastime.

His letter concludes:

That seems to be most of my news except to tell you I love you, I always have (since I met you) and always will. Yours forever and always, John.

A Little Bird Told Michael

Three-year-old Michael Witty wanted to see Nanna—Mrs R. Ellis, of Edward-st., Hessle—but he didn't know her address. Beauty, the budgie, told him and he set off alone for Hull bus station en route to Hessle.

MICHAEL WITTY, three-year-old son of Mr and Mrs John Witty, suddenly disappeared while his mother was getting ready to take him out.

After a frantic search of the house and garden, she dashed down the road, in time to see him standing by a zebra crossing waiting to cross the road.

The following conversation ensued: "Hey, where do you think you're going?" "To see Nanna." "But you can't go alone." "Why not? I know I want a Hesslewood bus, and it's a dark blue one." "But you don't know where Nanna lives." "Yes I do. She's Mrs Ellis, 9, Edward-st., Hessle."

❖   ❖   ❖

AT THIS, mother was thunderstruck, for no one so far as she knew, had taught the little boy his grandmother's name and address.

"How do you know?" she asked. "Beauty told me," was the reply.

Beauty is Mrs Ellis's green budgerigar, who, like many of his fellows, has been taught to say his name and address—and even, when he remembers, his telephone number—in case he gets lost.

The child must have been listening to the bird while staying with his grandmother, and memorised the words.

❖   ❖   ❖

Michael with Beauty

Barbara in her maternity suit

201

John with Don, Dick and Dave in 1958

John, Michael and Hazel

Michael and Hazel

EPILOGUE

We have many happy memories to look back on, dearest, but we have still happier ones to look forward to, don't you think so? (Barbara)

Most love stories culminate in a marriage. John and Barbara's story almost begins with one, for they were married just months after they first met in 1953. However, their love story continued for many more years after 1958.

They did have a third child, and Barbara was overjoyed to be fully conscious for the birth this time. David was born in 1964, the year that they moved out of their first house in Hull and bought their first car. David and Michael inherited their father's interest in Science, both working in the pharmaceutical industry after graduating from Oxford. I became a teacher, following the career that my mother would have chosen if she had had the chance.

John spent the next thirty years as a lecturer at the Nautical College in Hull and as principal lecturer at what was then the University of Humberside and is now the University of Lincoln. The library was inevitably his responsibility. He was always referred to as Captain, although he was never Master of his own ship. He tested pilots navigating the channels and sand banks of the Humber estuary, and marked NVQ exams for apprentices long after he retired. The British Council sent him to Northern Spain, to Turkey and even to China, to share his expertise in setting up a degree course in Fishery Science.

He continued with his love of reading and of nature, seeking to educate himself on many different subjects. Despite his early scepticism, he became a Gideon, making presentations of the New Testament and Psalms to schoolchildren and talking to them about how he had read the Bible at sea. His practical skills were greatly in demand by his local church, where he held the role of churchwarden for many years.

Barbara was a devoted mother and then grandmother, but she also became increasingly involved in voluntary work. She supported and worked with abandoned single mothers and represented the Mothers' Union nationally on the Social Responsibility Panel. At the same time, she continued to be a well organised, energetic housewife and always looked immaculate.

After John retired, they travelled extensively, enabling Barbara to visit some of the far-flung places she had never seen.

John died unexpectedly of a pulmonary embolism in December 2003, just two weeks before they were due to celebrate their golden wedding with their family, which now included eight grandchildren.

Barbara lived with a broken heart for a further ten years, listening to children read in the local primary school, providing telephone counselling for the bereaved, always ready to provide afternoon tea and a listening ear to her many visitors. She was known as Grandma, not only to her own grandchildren but to their friends as well. Barbara finally died of heart failure in March 2013, sixty years after she first met John at the Mission in Hull.

Their gravestone bears the inscription '*Together in heavenly love abiding*'.

Ruby Wedding 1993

With grandchildren 1993

With children and grandchildren 1996

John and Barbara in their seventies, with Michael

APPENDIX

HIT SONGS OF THE 1950s

Chapter One

'Hold Me, Thrill Me, Kiss Me' by Muriel Smith peaked at number 3 in the UK in June 1953

'Getting to Know You' was a show tune from the 1951 musical 'The King and I'

'Somewhere Along the Way' by Nat King Cole reached number 2 ion the UK in November 1952

'Faith can Move Mountains' by Nat Kling Cole was UK number 10 in February 1953

'Till I Waltz again with you' by Teresa Brewer was number 1 in the USA in February and March 1953

'I Believe' by Frankie Laine was UK number 1 in April, July and August 1953

'All the Time and Everywhere' by Dickie Valentine was UK number 9 in March 1953

'Outside of Heaven' by Eddie Fisher topped the UK charts in January 1953

'Tell me a Story' by Jimmy Boyd and Frankie Lane was UK number 5 in May 1953

'In a Golden Coach' by Dickie Valentine celebrated the Coronation at number 3 in June 1953

'Downhearted' by Eddie Fisher was UK number 3 in May 1953

'Oh, Happy Day' by the Johnson Brothers was UK number 4 in April 1953

Chapter Two

'*Say You're Mine Again*' by Jane Hutton was UK number 6 in September 1953

'*Side by Side*' by Kay Starr was UK number 7 in May 1953

'*Eternally*' by Jimmy Young was UK number 8 in September 1953

Chapter Three

'*Smile (Though Your Heart is Aching)*' by Nat King Cole reached UK number 2 in October 1954

'*(Oh Baby Mine) I Get So Lonely*' by The Four Knights reached UK number 5 in July 1954

'*Little Things mean a lot*' by Kitty Kallen was UK number 1 in September 1954

'*Three Coins in the Fountain*' by Frank Sinatra was UK number 1 in September 1954

'*No One But You*' by Billy Eckstine reached UK number 3 in January 1955

'*There Must Be a Reason*' by Frankie Laine reached UK number 9 in October 1954

'*Rain, Rain, Rain*' by Frankie Laine reached UK number 8 in November 1954

'*This 'Ole House*' by Rosemary Clooney was UK number 1 in November 1954

'*Let's Get Together*' by The Big Ben Banjo Band reached UK number 6 in December 1954

'*Let's have another party*' by Winifred Atwell was UK number 1 in December 1954

Chapter Four

'*My son, My son*' by Vera Lynn was UK number 1 in November 1954

'*The Finger of Suspicion*' by Dickie Valentine was UK number 1 in January 1955

'*Dreamboat*' by Alma Cogan was UK number 1 in July 1955

'*Stranger in Paradise*' by Tony Bennett was UK number 1 in May 1955

'*Prize of Gold*' by Joan Regan reached UK number 6 in April 1955

'*Ev'ry Day of my Life*' by Malcolm Vaughan reached UK number 5 in September 1955

'*I wonder*' by Dickie Valentine reached UK number 4 in July 1955

'If You Believe' by Johnnie Ray reached UK number 7 in May 1955

'The Breeze and I' by Caterina Valente reached UK number 5 in September 1955

'Learnin' the Blues' by Frank Sinatra reached UK number 2 in September 1955

'Ready, Willing and Able' by Doris Day reached UK number 7 in April 1955

'Cool Water' by Frankie Laine reached UK number 2 in August 1955

'Strange Lady in Town' by Frankie Laine reached UK number 6 in August 1955

'I'll Come When You Call' by Ruby Murray reached UK number 6 in November 1955

Chapter Five

'Love Me or Leave Me' by Sammy Davis Jr reached UK number 8 in September 1955

'When You Lose the One You Love' by David Whitfield reached UK number 7 in December 1955

'Ain't That a Shame' by Pat Boone reached UK number 7 in December 1955

'Mr Sandman' by Dickie Valentine reached UK number 5 in February 1955

'Love is the Tender Trap' by Frank Sinatra reached UK number 2 in February 1956

'Only You (And You Alone)' by The Hilltoppers reached UK number 3 in May 1956

'Memories Are Made of This' by Dave King reached UK number 5 in March 1956

'See You Later Alligator' by Bill Haley and his Comets reached UK number 7 in March 1956

'Lost John' by Lonnie Donegan reached UK number 2 in June 1956

'Zambezi' by Lou Busch and his Orchestra reached UK number 2 in March 1956

'I'll be home' by Pat Boone was UK number 1 in June 1956

Chapter Six

'Heartbreak Hotel' by Elvis Presley reached UK number 2 in June 1956

'Why do fools fall in love?' by Frankie Lymon and the Teenagers was UK number 1 in July 1956

'Born to be with you' by The Chordettes reached UK number 8 in September 1958

'A Sweet Old-fashioned Girl' by Teresa Brewer reached UK number 3 in August 1956

'Whatever Will Be Will Be' by Doris Day was UK number 1 in August 1956

'The Wayward Wind' by Tex Ritter reached UK number 8 in August 1958

'Singing the Blues' was UK number 1 in January 1957, in versions by both Tommy Steele and Guy Mitchell

'A Woman in Love' by Frankie Laine was UK number 1 in October 1956

'Blue moon' by Elvis Presley reached UK number 9 in November 1956

'My prayer' by The Platters reached UK number 3 in November 1956

'Make it a party' by Winifred Atwell reached UK number 7 in January 1957

'Knee Deep in the Blues' by Guy Mitchell reached UK number 3 in March 1957

'The girl can't help it' by Little Richard reached UK number 9 in April 1957

'Baby, Baby' by Frankie Lymon and the Teenagers reached UK number 4 in May 1957

'Look Homeward, Angel' by Johnnie Ray reached UK number 7 in April 1957

'Around the World' was a UK hit for Gracie Fields, Bing Crosby and Ronnie Hilton in June 1957

'When I Fall in Love' by Nat King Cole reached UK number 2 in May 1957

'Putting on the Style' by Lonnie Donegan was UK number 1 in June 1957

'Too much' by Elvis Presley with The Jordanaires reached UK number 6 in June 1957

'Don't forbid me' by Pat Boone reached UK number 2 in March 1957

Chapter Seven

'Bye Bye Love' by The Everly Brothers reached UK number 6 inSeptember 1957

'That'll be the Day' by The Crickets was UK number 1 in November 1957

'My Special Angel' by Malcolm Vaughan was UK number 3 in January 1958

'Whole Lotta Woman' by Marvin Rainwater was UK number 1 in April 1958

'*Let's have a Ball*' by Winifred Atwell reached UK number 4 in January 1958

'*Oh Boy!*' by Buddy Holly and The Crickets reached UK number 3 in January 1958

'*La Dee Dah*' by Jackie Dennis reached UK number 4 in 1958

'*Who's sorry now?*' by Connie Francis was UK number 1 in May 1958

'*Alone*' by Petula Clark reached UK number 8 in December 1957

'*The Story of my Life*' by Michael Holliday was UK number 1 in February 1958

'*Maybe Baby*' by Buddy Holly and The Crickets reached UK number 4 in April 1958

'*I love you baby*' by Paul Anka was UK number 3 in December 1957

'*It's too soon to know*' by Pat Boone reached UK number 7 in May 1958

'*A Wonderful Time up there*' by Pat Boone reached UK number 2 in May 1958

'*On the Street where you live*' by Vic Damone was UK number 1 in June 1958

'*Rave on*' by Buddy Holly reached UK number 5 in August 1958